this map shows, but southern Africa, the Pacific and the Americas were unknown.

Johanna Bekt

DISCOVERERS

OF THE NEW WORLD

ILLUSTRATED WITH MAPS, PAINTINGS, PRINTS,

AND DRAWINGS OF THE PERIOD

SPAIN
Columbus
Vespucci, Balboa, Magellan
Cortés, Pizarro
Ponce de León, Cabeza de Vaca
Coronado, De Soto

PORTUGAL
Cabral

RUSSIA
Bering

PORTUGAL   RUSSIA   SPAIN

ENGLAND
Cabot
Gilbert, Frobisher, Davis
Waymouth, Drake, Cook

NETHERLANDS
Hudson

FRANCE
Verrazano, Cartier, Champlain
Marquette, Jolliet, La Salle

DISCOVERERS

OF THE NEW WORLD

by the editors of AMERICAN HERITAGE
The Magazine of History

FRANCE NETHERLANDS ENGLAND

narrative by JOSEF BERGER

in consultation with LAWRENCE C. WROTH

Librarian Emeritus John Carter Brown Library
Brown University, Providence, Rhode Island

PUBLISHED BY

AMERICAN HERITAGE PUBLISHING CO., INC.

NEW YORK

BOOK TRADE DISTRIBUTION BY

GOLDEN PRESS · NEW YORK

FOREWORD

THE LONG SUCCESSION of explorations across perilous seas, along uncharted coasts, and through unknown interiors which forms the subject of the book before us extends from the late fifteenth to the late eighteenth century, from the middle years of the Renaissance to the beginning of the Industrial Revolution. This record of nearly three centuries of great and less great expeditions seems to us, in looking back, one of the most exciting and most revelatory periods in the whole reach of world history. In the course of it, the physical horizons of European man were immeasurably widened and, as a consequence, his concept of the world in which he lived was enlarged almost beyond recognition in the fields of politics, economics, social relations, and religious concepts. The narratives of the voyages of discovery and exploration, through which was brought about this change from the mediaeval to the modern world, created a species of historical writing made up of firsthand personal accounts direct from the pens of the great captains or of trustworthy associates in their adventures.

Together these narratives—beginning with the first letter of Columbus in 1493—recorded explorations by sea and land which fixed the location upon the globe of the previously unknown American continents, outlined their shape, estimated their size, and brought into unity the scattered elements discovered piecemeal through years of uncoordinated voyaging. It is from these personal, firsthand accounts of the explorers, stripped down to the barest statement of their achievement, that the rugged adventure in which all western Europe engaged is presented to us in Josef Berger's book. In his narrative we follow the successive thrusts into the unknown through which the ends of the Earth were tied together and North, South, East, and West were brought into a comprehensible relationship.

Mr. Berger's story of the great discoveries, explorations, and conquests has been written for young people in clear, straightforward language, without any degree of oversimplification. This admirable approach has made his book one which adults also will be able to read with a sense of revelation. It is hardly necessary to comment upon the immediately perceptible fact that the illustrations which adorn and clarify the text open still wider the door of enlightenment to young and old.

LAWRENCE C. WROTH

LIBRARY OF CONGRESS CATALOGUE CARD NUMBER: 60–10300

Navigation is being taught with globes, hour-glasses, cross-staves, astrolabe, and dividers in this picture taken from a Dutch book of the seventeenth century.

CONTENTS

THE SECRET

America was once the biggest secret on earth. The New World—the great belt of two continents hitched across the western half of the globe—is four times as large as Europe. Yet 500 years ago the greatest geographers in Europe did not know it existed.

This was true even though some Europeans had actually been here. Nearly ten centuries ago the Vikings ventured across the North Atlantic Ocean—Norway to Iceland to Greenland to North America—and stayed a few years. Now and then, crews of far-ranging fishermen from other parts of Europe may have beheld the land. But none of these people understood how vast it was, or how important.

Geographers of the fifteenth century believed there was only a scattering of islands in the ocean all the way from Spain westward to China. And, of course, they did not dream of such a thing as the mighty Pacific Ocean, lying west beyond the two continents—twice as large as the Atlantic.

These learned men knew the earth was not flat, that it had the shape of a ball. If they had wanted to show the outlines of its surface, they would have drawn the Atlantic Ocean much wider than it really is,

Marco Polo sets out from Venice, Italy, in 1271, on his famous journey to China.

*Twenty-four years later he returned to Europe, where he
wrote a book telling of the gold and jewels of the East.*

After Marco Polo (left) told them of the wealth of China, other Europeans tried to find sea routes to the East Indies.

for China, Japan, and the Spice Islands of the Far East. But nobody had tried going to reach the Indies by sailing westward. Sailors spoke of the Atlantic with dread. Like the Romans, who had called it *Mare Tenebrosum*, they called it the "Sea of Darkness." Nobody knew what storms, what menacing shoals, what giant sea serpents or other terrors might be lurking in it. And few sailors cared to find out.

If a traveler wanted to go to the Indies, he would have to turn eastward and proceed overland to distant Persia and then travel thousands of miles through Asia, over high mountains, across burning desert sands, and along lonely roads where bandits lay in wait.

Only a few adventurers—like Marco Polo—had ever made that trip. And yet, Europe was always buzzing with talk of the Indies. Wondrous tales were told—many true enough—of the splendors, the golden roofs and spices of the Orient, with its teeming cities, busy docks, and warehouses bulging with luxuries.

The Indies were talked about in Europe because they produced many of the good things of life that Europeans longed for and could not buy anywhere else.

and they would have stretched the continent of Asia around to the eastward many thousands of miles beyond its actual limit so as to bring its shores to the Atlantic. Gazing out to sea from Spain or Portugal, men believed that somewhere on the other side of that ocean lay Cathay, Cipangu, and the Indies—their names

The Mongol ruler, Kublai Khan, was emperor of Cathay during Polo's visit.

Rich people had pepper on the table and other rare flavorings in the kitchen. They dressed in silks. They wore jewelry. Some owned rubies and strings of pearls. All these things came from the Indies. From the Far East they were carried by ships and caravans of camels from one trader to another. They were bought and sold, again and again, as they moved slowly from one country to the next, until finally they reached Europe.

Then there came a time, in the middle of the fifteenth century, when the flow of these goods was choked off. The main overland trade route was closed.

This had happened when the Turks, who had been fighting the Christians for centuries, marched into the Christian city of Constantinople and seized it, in 1453. Up

Contantinople (below) fell to the Turks 39 years before Columbus' voyage.

until then, goods from the Indies, on their way to Europe, had had to pass through Constantinople, since the Turks had already cut off all other land routes. At last they would let nothing go through Constantinople, either.

A few men—makers of maps, readers of books, and watchers of stars—began to ask themselves how the Indies might best be reached by sea. That question proved to be the beginning of a search that was to spread to many far places and to go on for hundreds of years.

It was really a search of the earth. As it went on it brought vast changes, into the lives of people and of great nations. It decided many important questions—for example, the very important one as to what kind of America we were to be born in, or

Prince Henry the Navigator of Portugal (above) helped explorers who were trying to find a sea route to the Indies. In 1375, a French book telling of Polo's travels, carried this imaginative picture (below) of pepper-gatherers in Asia.

*These wooden panels are part of a Spanish map of the world, painted in 1375,
which is known as the Catalan Atlas. Turn the book upside down to see (upper
right) the caravan of men and camels. This is thought to picture Marco Polo's
father, Niccolò, and his uncle, Maffeo, meeting the envoys of Kublai Khan on the
Polos' journey to Cathay in 1266, five years before young Marco left Venice.*

Vasco da Gama

by sea. But the known routes on their maps did not reach very far. Beyond a few hundred miles, men's knowledge grew vague.

One of these suggested routes was southward along the coast of Africa. In 1415 bold sailors from Portugal, inspired and directed by Prince Henry the Navigator, had begun edging down that way. If Africa ended somewhere, so that they could sail around it, then they could continue across the Indian Ocean and on to the Far East.

The first man to reach the East by sea by this route was Vasco da Gama, who sailed from Lisbon in 1497 with four ships, rounded Africa's Cape of Good Hope, and made the port of Calicut, India, in 1498.

perhaps whether we would be living in America at all today!

Those fifteenth century map makers believed that from Europe there were two ways to go to the Indies

The other route—so the map makers believed—lay across the Atlantic. The Portuguese had sailed westward a thousand miles out on

Calicut, on the west coast of India, as it appeared in 1573. Da Gama had landed

the Atlantic to discover and colonize the Azores. But no one had yet dared to cross the Sea of Darkness which lay westward beyond those islands.

None dared until, in 1492, three little ships, commanded by Christopher Columbus, set out from Spain, paused at the Canary Islands, then pushed on and on into the long emptiness of the unknown sea.

With the passing of a few more years, a few more voyages, Europe came to face the truth that the land Columbus had found was *not* the Indies. Instead, it was a New World —a barrier that actually stood in the way of that great goal.

Like ants, then, that suddenly find their line of march blocked by an unexpected wall, the adventurers from the Old World began to spread along the length of North and South America, trying to find a way through to the Orient. They searched inlets, bays, and rivers, looking for a strait that lead to the Indies.

Slowly they learned how enormous the New World barrier was. For thousands of miles, as far as they could dig into the northern wastes, as deep as they dared probe to the south, there it lay before them, solid, impassable.

Their search led them to the discovery of two huge continents. Bit by bit they explored the shore lines of North and South America until their outlines were complete. To do this, they sometimes had to throw their very lives into the gamble to get at the truth. It took them more than 300 years. But it would be hard to imagine anything more exciting than the events which occurred after men from Europe stepped ashore on what they thought to be the Indies and instead ran head on into the mighty secret of America.

here 75 years before—the first European to sail around Africa to India.

THE SEA OF DARKNESS

Christopher Columbus

Christopher Columbus' great adventure in 1492 is exciting not so much because it happened but because it might never have happened at all. So many things might have prevented his discovery of America—and so many almost did!

Columbus had read a fascinating account of the Indies in the book of Marco Polo, an Italian who had journeyed to Cathay by the eastward, overland route in 1275, two centuries earlier. It had taken Polo three years to get there. Since the world was known to be round, Columbus wondered if it would not be much easier and much shorter to try to reach the East by sea—sailing westward across the Atlantic?

After that he studied every book and map touching on the subject. He wrote a letter to a man who was reputed to know more about geography than anyone else in the world. This man, called "Master Paul, the Physician," was Paolo Toscanelli, an astronomer of Florence, Italy. Columbus revealed his plan. What did Dr. Toscanelli think of it?

Toscanelli replied: The plan was "noble and grand." If he reached the Indies, as he should within 5,000 miles, said Toscanelli (a mistaken guess which more than halved the distance between Portugal and China), Christopher Columbus would certainly be honored by all the world. And the doctor sent along a map of the known world.

But a scholar's backing was not the backing of a nation. Columbus must have ships and sailors. And for these the only people he could go to were kings and queens.

There his troubles began. He first discussed his plan in 1484, with King John of Portugal. After months of waiting, Columbus was refused.

Then he tried Spain. King Ferdinand and Queen Isabella listened to him, but they must consult their ad-

Columbus' signature (below) probably abbreviates the Greek and Latin
phrase: Servus Sum Altissimi Salvatoris,
Χριστός, Mariae, Ὑιός—Χρoferens, or, "I
am Christopher, servant of the Most
High Saviour, Christ, Son of Mary."

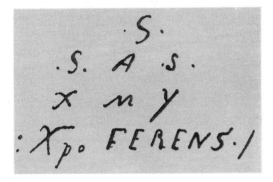

Columbus' coat of arms (above) made in
1502, pictures a group of islands, sig-
nifying his discovery of America. Its
motto read: "Columbus found the New
World for Spain." The drawing (below)
copies Martin Behaim's globe, made in
1491. The oldest globe in existence, it
may have been known to Columbus before his first voyage. It does not show
America, and puts Cipangu (Japan) in
the Atlantic between Europe and Asia.

visors. Columbus waited six years to
get an answer, and again he was refused. But after Columbus had already set out for France, in an attempt to interest the French king in
western exploration, a powerful
official of the Spanish court named
Luis de Santangel advised Isabella
to change her mind. She did, and sent
a messenger to find Columbus. He
was four miles out of town when the
Queen's courier caught up with him.

And so it was that by a last-minute
decision, the dwindling chance of the
great adventure was saved.

At the little town of Palos, in
southwest Spain, Columbus by royal
order, was given two tiny caravels,
the *Niña* and the *Pinta*, and a small
ship, or *nao*, which Columbus char-
tered himself—the *Santa María*.

Now he must have men. The
townsfolk earned their living as
sailors and fishermen but the sailors
of Palos wanted no part of Columbus' voyage.

Again the enterprise was in danger, until a sea captain stepped in to
save it. Martín Alonso Pinzón was
one of the smartest skippers in that
whole corner of Spain. He liked Co-

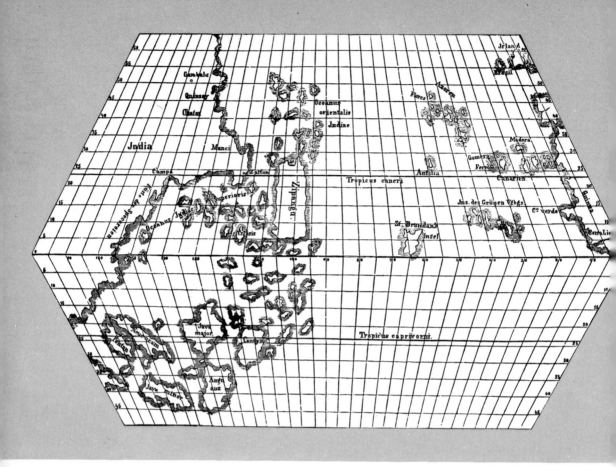

This is a restored version of the map Toscanelli sent Columbus in 1481. Like the Behaim globe, it places Zipangu (Japan) near where America was to be discovered.

lumbus' scheme. Here was their chance, he said, to make some money! The Queen was offering a cash reward to the first sailor to see land. And Columbus was promising that every man who signed up would share in some part of the profits.

Still the sailors refused to sign on. But then they learned that Martín Alonzo Pinzón was going—Columbus had chosen him to be captain of the *Pinta*—and so were Pinzón's two brothers. Since the Pinzóns were men of influence, one by one, a crew of ninety sailors volunteered.

It took months to get the little fleet fitted out shipshape. Nobody knows

the exact dimensions of the ships, but certainly the largest of the three, the *Santa María*, was not much more than 100 feet from stem to stern, and perhaps not that long. The *Santa María* probably weighed less than 100 tons, the *Niña* 55 tons, and the *Pinta* 60 tons. Ten *Santa Marías* lined up in a row would not have reached from bow to stern of today's largest ocean liner.

The design of these vessels was excellent—the work of builders who had been experimenting and improving for generations—and they were all seaworthy and fast.

At last, early on the morning of

August 3, 1492, *Adelante* (or Captain General) Columbus gave the order to get underway and the three little vessels with ninety-four people on board sailed from Palos.

On the third day at sea the *Pinta's* rudder slipped out of its slot and broke, making it impossible to steer. Captain Martín Alonso Pinzón strapped it up as best he could, and on went the fleet.

Columbus stayed five weeks on the Canary Islands, doing his best to find another ship to replace the *Pinta*. Finding none, he had a new rudder built for her, and resumed the voyage.

As the little fleet passed the island of Ferro, westernmost of the Canaries, a hush fell over the men.

Many prayed. They had reached "the end of the world," and ahead lay the great Sea of Darkness.

Out on the open ocean, Columbus picked up the steady wind, always blowing from the northeast, that he had observed in his earlier days of sailing off the coast of Africa. Today we call it the trade wind. And it brought good sailing indeed—in ten days, nearly 1,200 miles!

In those days there was no way to measure distance sailed, except to watch the water and then estimate the ship's speed. But distances and directions were matters Columbus was not eager to have anybody know but himself. Information about the route to the Indies might be worth something later on. For another thing, the men were sure to be frightened if the Indies did not appear where he had said they would. So each day he gave the men a figure which was less than his honest guess as to their actual mileage, and for himself he kept a secret record of what he thought was the true distance.

For days and weeks they sailed through the Sargasso Sea, an enormous brown patch of gulfweed—a floating seaweed which made the ocean look like a limitless meadow. At night, its awesome phosphorescent glow flickered about the ships.

They saw many things which they

No pictures of any of Columbus' ships exist; but the Santa María *probably resembled this vessel, drawn in 1493.*

thought were signs of land—land birds, and cloud formations which often signified land.

Early in October, after a month on the open ocean, it was clear to all hands that they had sailed more than 2,400 miles—the distance Columbus had estimated to Japan—although Japan is actually 10,600 air miles west of Lisbon.

Had they missed Japan? From that time on, fear took hold of Columbus himself. His course had been due west. But now great flocks of birds were passing over the ships, all going west southwest. Columbus decided to follow them, and gave the order to the helmsman to change course from west to west southwest.

On October 10, the ships were two hundred miles from land—only one more good day's sailing. But the men, not knowing this, gathered around Columbus and told him they had had all they could stand. They demanded that he turn back.

Nobody knows exactly what was said on board the *Santa María* in that tense moment when the future of the world was being decided. In his diary, Columbus wrote only that he tried to cheer up the men as much as he could, reminding them of the advantages they might gain, and adding that however much they might complain, he had to go to the Indies and that he would go on until he found that part of the world "with the help of our Lord." And mutiny was staved off.

This map, painted on calfskin, is owned by the Bibliothèque Nationale, in Paris, France. It is believed by some scholars that it was drawn by Columbus, and that it may have been used aboard the Santa María in 1492.

Since Africa's Cape of Good Hope is present, this map could not have been made until after its discovery in 1488; and as America is missing, it was probably drawn before Columbus' return to Europe in 1493. The rings at left show the Earth at the center of the Solar System—for men did not know the Earth revolved about the sun until after 1543, when the new theory of Copernicus was first published.

Now the ships were running before a spanking good breeze, which next day rose to a gale and sent them racing west southwest.

On the morning of October 11, the men were certain land was nearby. They saw new signs floating in the water—a branch of a shrub with

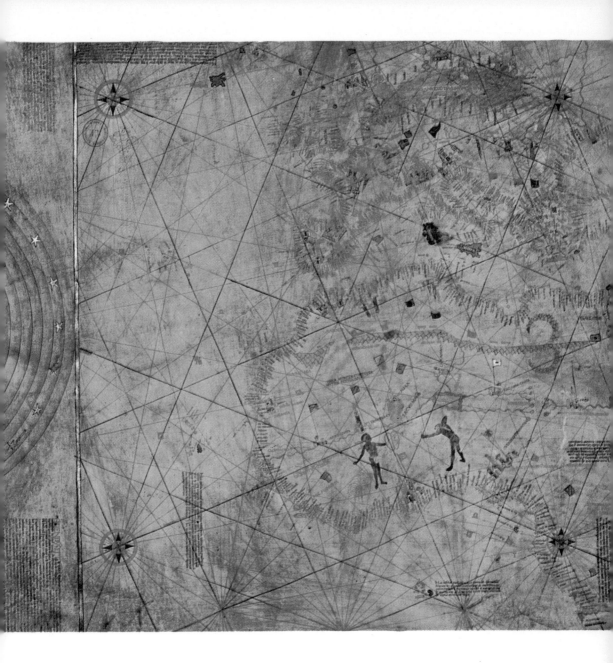

leaves and berries on it, a board, a wooden staff that had been hand-carved. Hour by hour the sailors' excitement rose.

Each man hoped to be the one to claim the Queen's reward—worth about $200 a year for life, a princely sum to those poor fellows!

At sunset Columbus did a strange thing. Suddenly he gave an order to change the course back to due west! If it was just a hunch it was a good one because it put him in a straight line for the nearest land.

Nobody wanted to go to sleep that night. The men clung to the rail of

23

The drawing (above) shows a 16th century navigator sighting the sun with a cross-staff. The angle of the sun's inclination could be read off a scale on the staff (below) once the large arm was lined up with the sun and the horizon.

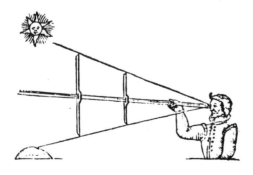

the *Santa María* as she went plunging along before the gale, all eyes straining into the darkness ahead, trying to sight land. Some sailors climbed into the rigging.

A little ahead they could see the *Niña*, her lights winking and bobbing on the black, turbulent water. And a little ahead of her, the *Pinta* was leading the way.

At ten o'clock Columbus, standing on the sterncastle of the *Santa María*, declared he had just seen

This painting shows Columbus being rowed out to the Santa María *at dawn, just before he set sail from the little town of Palos de la Frontera, Spain, on August 3, 1492, at the beginning of his historic voyage to America. Actually, the Admiral of the Ocean Sea (or Adelante, as Columbus was called) sailed before sunrise.*

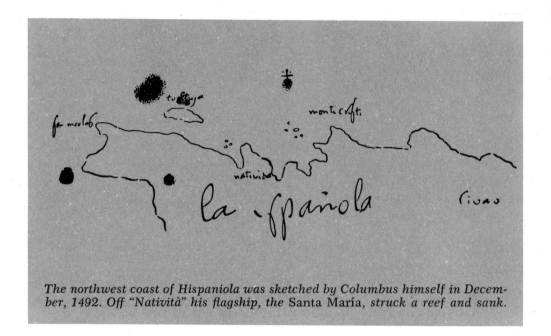

The northwest coast of Hispaniola was sketched by Columbus himself in December, 1492. Off "Natività" his flagship, the Santa María, *struck a reef and sank.*

something—a little flicker of light in the distance, such as a candle might give off. Then it was gone.

Excitement may have made him imagine it. Certainly it could not have been land, which at that hour was still too far away.

At eleven o'clock the moon rose astern. It was nearly full. Now the men could see a long way ahead. Three hours more, the little ships sped on, with still no shore sighted. Then, at two o'clock in the morning, October 12, 1492, a sailor on the *Pinta*, Rodrigo de Triana, cried out from his place atop the forecastle:

"Tierra! Tierra! Land!"

In a few minutes everyone could make it out—far across the water, the white of a moonlit beach, like a thin ribbon of silver on the horizon.

The ships took in sail. Men tried to shout above the wind, rail to rail. Rough voices of sailors joined clum-

The Indian chief, Guacanagarí, arrives at Fort Navidad, carried in a litter. He had helped Columbus salvage timbers from the ship, from which the fort was built.

sily in a hymn. Some could not even try to sing. They were weeping.

The Queen of Spain's reward for the first man to sight land went to Columbus—on the flimsy ground that he had seen a light four hours before Rodrigo de Triana sang out.

Dawn of Saturday, October 13, brought Columbus the surprise of his life. On the shore where he expected to find great cities and a wealthy civilization, he beheld people running around "as naked as when their mothers bore them."

As the Spaniards stepped ashore on Guanahaní (or Iguana Island)—the island that Columbus named San Salvador—the Arawak Indians who lived there gathered on the beach but timidly kept their distance. Of this first meeting Columbus wrote:

"That we might become friends I gave some of them red caps and others necklaces of glass beads—nothing of much value but nevertheless things that gave them great delight and made them so friendly toward us that it was a marvelous thing to see.

"After we had gone back to the ship's boats they swam out to us and brought parrots, skeins of cotton yarn, and such trifles as they owned, and we traded small bells and other trinkets for them."

Their skin was neither black nor white, he wrote, but rather like that of the Canary Islanders. "They neither carry such weapons as guns and swords nor know anything about them. When I showed them our swords they took hold of them by the blade and cut themselves." Hoping he had reached the Indies, he called these people Indians.

Later he wrote that they came out to the ships in canoes, "which are made out of the trunk of a tree, all of one piece and wonderfully worked. Some are very large, holding as many as forty-five men."

Their houses were made like booths, some quite large, "and looking like tents in a camp without regular streets."

By nature, Columbus found, these islanders were extremely timid. They knew nothing of war. They spoke of

Columbus left some of the crew of the Santa María *at Navidad, and sailed back to Spain. After he left, Indians killed his men, and laid the fortress in ruins.*

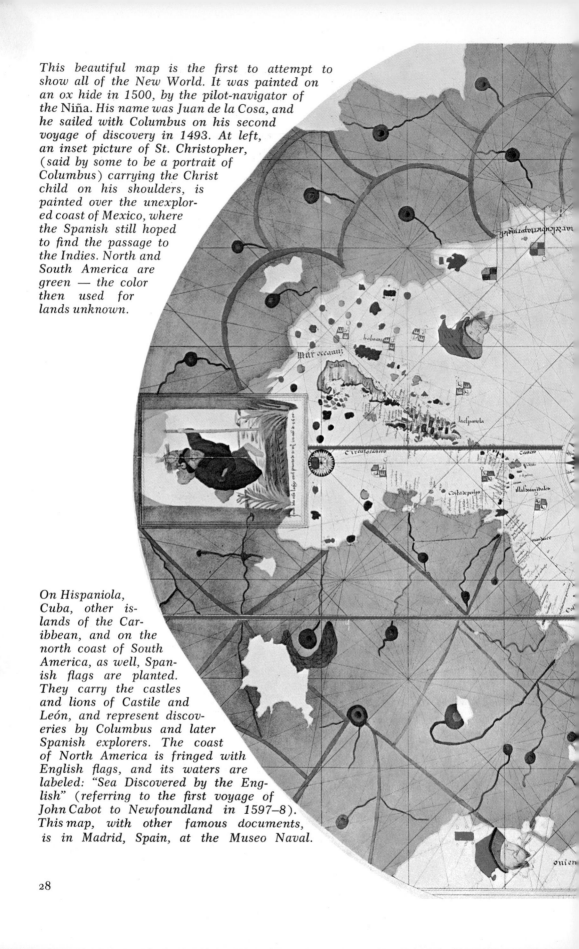

This beautiful map is the first to attempt to show all of the New World. It was painted on an ox hide in 1500, by the pilot-navigator of the Niña. His name was Juan de la Cosa, and he sailed with Columbus on his second voyage of discovery in 1493. At left, an inset picture of St. Christopher, (said by some to be a portrait of Columbus) carrying the Christ child on his shoulders, is painted over the unexplored coast of Mexico, where the Spanish still hoped to find the passage to the Indies. North and South America are green — the color then used for lands unknown.

On Hispaniola, Cuba, other islands of the Caribbean, and on the north coast of South America, as well, Spanish flags are planted. They carry the castles and lions of Castile and León, and represent discoveries by Columbus and later Spanish explorers. The coast of North America is fringed with English flags, and its waters are labeled: "Sea Discovered by the English" (referring to the first voyage of John Cabot to Newfoundland in 1597–8). This map, with other famous documents, is in Madrid, Spain, at the Museo Naval.

28

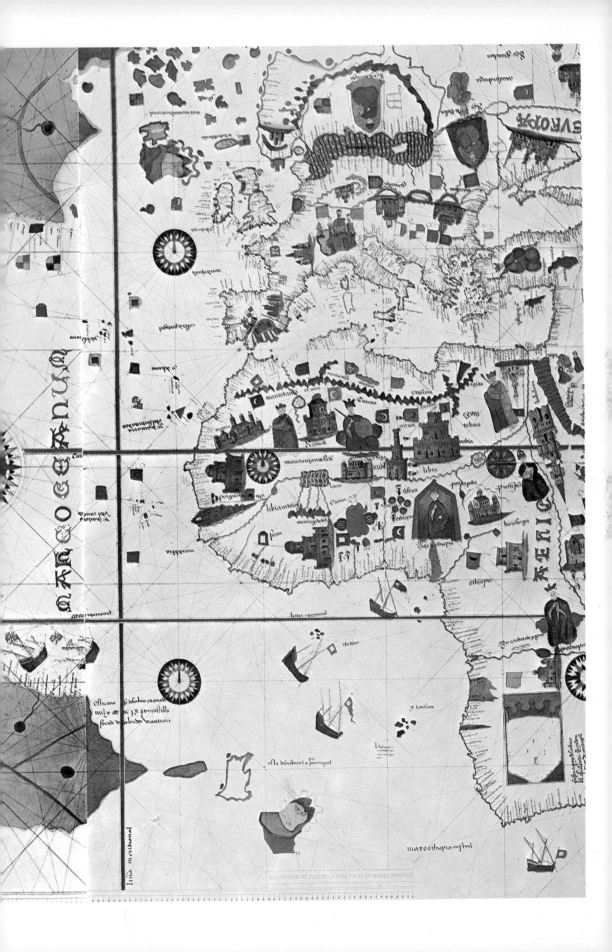

insula hyspana

American Indians were pictured for Europeans in 1493, in this early view of Columbus' ship arriving at Hispaniola.

the Spaniards—with their huge bird-like ships, their mirrors and guns—as "men from Heaven." They talked of their enemies—a tribe on another island, who sometimes raided them, carried them off, and ate them. These were the Caribs, from whom we get the name Caribbean; and sometimes they were called the Canibs, from which we get our word *cannibal*.

But they themselves were innocent and peaceable, Columbus wrote, and he added, "Fifty Spaniards could subjugate this entire people."

In the years that followed, when the Spanish came to settle the West Indies they enslaved these Indians. Hundreds of thousands were worked to death, tortured, or killed outright. In 1490, about 300,000 Arawak (or

Taino) Indians lived on Hispaniola. After more than fifty years of Spanish rule, in 1548, there were only 500 Indians left on the island.

For three months Columbus searched among the islands of America for something that looked like China or Japan. He looked especially eagerly for gold and spices.

He seized a few Indians, tried to make them understand what he wanted, and let them be his guides. They led him to Cuba, then to Hispaniola. There he found small bits of gold, and on Hispaniola, he guessed correctly, there were gold mines.

But where were the many-towered cities of the great Khan of Cathay whom Marco Polo had written about, the busy markets, the teeming seaports? Columbus heard the Indians speak of a powerful ruler who had much gold and they called him "Kami." This, he decided, was their way of pronouncing *Khan*. And he changed his mind and thought it must be China after all. And so, back and forth, Columbus switched his ideas as he went from island to island, trying to make himself believe he had found countries that lay on the other side of the earth!

One night as the *Santa María* was sailing off the coast of Hispaniola, the helmsman wanted to steal a nap. He told the ship's boy to take the rudder.

Except for the boy, all hands were asleep. Suddenly the lad cried out. The ship had run upon a hidden bar. She was held fast until the sea opened her seams. Columbus wept when the *Santa María* had to be abandoned. Now, with only two ships and more men than they could hold, Columbus decided to build a fort on the island, leave part of the crew there to settle and hunt for gold, and go on himself in the *Niña*.

He kept looking for the Indies until the middle of January. Then, having found nothing resembling those countries, he sail for home.

The trip back proved more dangerous than the westward crossing. Fine sailing, with a strong west wind, took the *Niña* and the *Pinta* to a point south of the Azores. Then, in mid-February, one of the most tempestuous winters ever known on the Atlantic overtook them.

For days the *Niña* lived from minute to minute through storms "so shaking and straining her that she was in danger of being stove in or swamped." The ships lost each other.

Columbus was afraid both the *Niña* and the *Pinta* would go down. The world would never hear the great news he had for it. The thought was more than he could bear. Desperately he scrawled a statement on a piece of parchment, wrapped it watertight, sealed it in a keg, and threw the keg into the sea, in the hope that if he were lost, it would drift ashore and be found— but it disappeared forever.

Yet the stout little *Niña* kept afloat and found refuge at the island of Santa Maria, one of the Azores. These islands belonged to Portugal. And here Columbus narrowly escaped being arrested and imprisoned by the Portuguese.

He managed to get away, only to encounter a hurricane which ripped the *Niña's* sails to shreds and might have sent her to the bottom if Columbus had not been the great sailor that he was. At last he sighted the coast of Portugal, and at the coming of daylight saw his chance to escape

31

The waterfront of Lisbon, Portugal, must have looked much like this to Columbus when he landed here on March 4, 1493, on his return from his voyage to America.

the mountainous seas by running over a sand bar into the sheltered waters of the Tagus River, near the city of Lisbon.

Her crew rushed ashore. To the astonished watchers they blurted out that they had crossed the sea and found the Indies. To prove it they exhibited their Indian captives. Immediately news of the discovery swept along shore.

Columbus did not know just what would happen when he stepped on Portuguese soil. Would King John try to stop him, hide him away in a dungeon perhaps, and cheat Spain of the fruits of the discovery?

But if King John had wanted to do anything about it, it was too late now. The news was out. He swallowed any bitterness he may have felt towards this man whose scheme he himself had once rejected, treated Columbus politely, offered to help repair the battered *Niña*, and sent the returning hero on his way.

Several days later, the *Niña* dropped anchor in the harbor at Palos carrying presents of parrots and Indians for their Catholic Majesties, Ferdinand and Isabella of Spain. The ship had sailed away 224 days before on the greatest voyage of all time.

And thus, through an adventure that had run into one close call after another, the civilized world learned that a strange new land—a land which would soon be named America—lay on the other side of the Sea of Darkness.

Columbus risked landing in Portugal— then hostile to Spain—to escape a storm.

These cannibal Indians of Brazil were drawn from hearsay by a German in 1505.

THE NEW WORLD

Three more times Columbus came to America, still looking for China. The mystery of why China was not there haunted him, filled him with sadness, while at the same time the land that he had found, land of a thousand spells, unfolded its beauty before his wondering eyes.

Wherever he went—to Cuba, Puerto Rico, Jamaica, South America, down the coast of Central America to Panama—always it was the same story: instead of cities, the vast wilderness; instead of gold-plated palaces, grass huts and palm-leaf tents; instead of silk-robed merchant princes, "Indians" who did not have so much as a shirt to their backs.

At times he became reconciled to the truth that this land was not China, not Japan, not the Spice Islands, but some part of the earth that the learned geographers of Europe had never heard of before. It was "another world,"—and he called it exactly that. But he also insisted, until he died, that he had reached Asia.

Just a few days before he left Spain on the voyage that took him to South America, an exciting thing happened on the other side of the world. Vasco da Gama, a Portuguese navigator, sailed into the harbor of Calicut,

India. He had sailed east across the Indian Ocean, the first European to reach India by sailing around Africa's Cape of Good Hope.

The Portuguese did not believe Columbus had reached the Indies but they were very much interested in finding out just what it was he *had* reached. They wanted to see for themselves. The King and Queen of Spain—trying to keep their rival, Portugal, out—appealed to the Pope at Rome for the exclusive right to this new seaway.

The Pope settled the question by picking out a spot on the map about 1,500 miles west of the Cape Verde Islands, drawing a line up and down through it, and ruling that Spain was to have everything west of the line, Portugal everything east of it.

The line gave the bulge of Brazil to Portugal. It also left to Portugal a part of North America, but only because the map maker had mistakenly put it east of the line. All other parts of America were to belong to Spain.

A few years later, however, when England and France had entered the race in earnest for new territory, they challenged the right of any one person or group to divide up the earth. When the old Spanish-Portuguese division was cited as a reason for keeping France out of the new-found lands, King Francis I asked, "I should much like to see Adam's will and learn how he divided the earth."

If the New World was not the Indies, what was it? This was the ques-

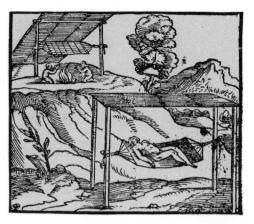

Hammocks, or hamacas, *invented by the Indians of Venezuela, were soon duplicated by the Spanish for use on shipboard.*

Eight Carib Indians operate this large sailing raft. Behind them, two Indians in dugout canoes are fishing with a net.

Rather than accept Christianity and work as slaves in Spanish gold mines, many Carib Indians killed themselves.

In May, 1493, Pope Alexander VI (top, left) ordered the unknown lands of the world divided between King John of Portugal (top, right) and King Ferdinand and Queen Isabella of Spain (below). The Treaty of Tordesillas (see map on page 84) signed by the two countries, finally fixed the location of the line.

tion confronting Columbus, and the great discoverer died without finding the answer. The nearest he could come to it was his belief that the land he had found was somewhere *near* the Indies, perhaps even attached in places; that it stood in the way of ships trying to reach China; and that somewhere a channel might be found, a strait that would enable the ships to get through.

To find such a strait was the purpose of his last voyage—just as it was of a number of men who followed him to America for centuries afterwards.

Before that search began, Columbus' feat in crossing the Atlantic was enough in itself to arouse the ambitions of other men. Now many a mariner dreamed of being the one to reach Cathay over the westward seaway. Five years after his first voyage, Columbus complained that "there is not a man, down to the very tailors, who does not beg to be allowed to become a discoverer!"

Some of those who tried it, however, were really great navigators. One of the greatest was Giovanni Caboto, who was born in Columbus' home town of Genoa, Italy. Because he went to England and sailed under the British flag, he became known as John Cabot.

Cabot was no mere imitator of Columbus. He had worked out his own plan for crossing the Atlantic Ocean long before Columbus' first voyage. As a dealer in spices in the Arabian city of Mecca he became curious about where those spices were coming from. When he questioned the traders they did not know; but they did say that the caravans which had brought them had come a very long way, and they had got them from other caravans which had also come a very long way, and so on.

These caravans traveled west and south. Therefore, John Cabot reasoned, if he wanted to go the other way around the world to the place where the spices came from (and it might be the shortest way) he would have to sail west and *north*. It was an exciting idea and John Cabot wanted very much to try it.

On the water front of the city of Bristol, England, were men who knew much about the North Atlantic—sailors who had been to Iceland on trading voyages. Cabot went to Bristol. He was there, in 1495, discussing it with mariners and shippers, when the news came to England of Columbus' success in "reaching the Indies."

In London there was much talk —about lands beyond the Western Ocean—in the shipping offices, the counting houses, and the court of King Henry VII. Two years later when John Cabot came to London with his proposition to try to reach the Indies, the King readily assented. This was easy, because Cabot was not asking for money. The merchants of Bristol had already agreed to give him what he needed.

This was little indeed—one ship, the *Matthew*, and eighteen men. He sailed from Bristol on May 2, 1497, and nearly eight weeks later, on June 24, sighted land.

It may have been the coast of Labrador, though more likely it was Newfoundland or Nova Scotia. The English claimed it as their "newe-founde land." But if Cabot wrote any

Sebastian Cabot's map of 1544 pictures the Gulf of St. Lawrence, which John Cabot, his father, discovered in 1497.

Sebastian with him. But this time he did not come back. Again there was no logbook, no written record. In 1939—nearly 500 years later—a document was found that reported John Cabot had gone down with his ship. How it happened, or where, is still unknown.

The son did come back. Sebastian Cabot talked a great deal, but mostly about himself. He claimed for himself the credit that his father had earned, even for making the first voyage. It was not until investigations were made by experts long after his death that the truth was learned about the discovery of the North American mainland, and the honor

Sebastian Cabot

description of it, it was lost, for no record by Cabot himself of any part of this voyage exists today.

With five or six ships, Cabot sailed again the next year, taking his son

Globe on which the name "America" first appeared was made by Martin Waldseemüller in St. Dié, France, in 1507. It is printed on the bulge of Brazil, at far right.

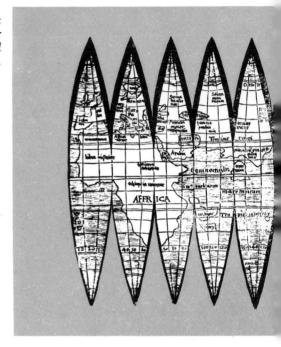

was shifted from Sebastian Cabot to John Cabot—the man Sebastian had tried to make the world forget.

While John Cabot was exploring Newfoundland, the Spanish continued probing the shores of the Caribbean. At one spot along the shore of Venezuela the sea yielded many oysters and the oysters yielded many pearls. The natives lived in huts built on stilts over the water ("Venezuela" is Spanish for "Little Venice") and inside those crude huts were pearls that had been gathered for generations, huge stores of jewels that would have been worth fortunes in Europe.

Columbus had heard about this pearl fishery from his Indian guides. Spaniards were excited by the report and other expeditions soon proved the Indians had told the truth. They brought back baskets full of pearls —"as common as chaff"—and they also took slaves by the shipload. On both items Spain enriched herself for many years.

First to seek out the pearls of Venezuela was Alonso de Ojeda, who had once served Columbus as captain of one of his ships. Using Columbus' map to guide him, Ojeda set sail from Spain in May, 1499, reached Venezuela and returned a year later. But more interesting to us now than the voyage itself, was one of the men who sailed with Ojeda—Amerigo Vespucci.

This is the first picture to show the landing of Columbus in the New World. It appeared in an edition of Vespucci's letters, printed in Italy in 1507.

40

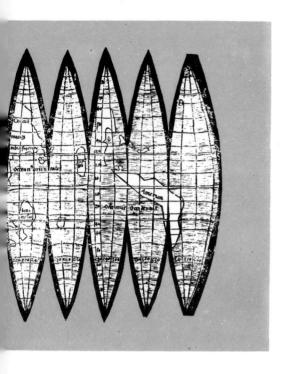

If names were very important, Americans probably would have insisted long ago that the name of their country be changed from the United States of America to the United States of Columbia. Since names are not that important, they have accepted an accident of history which has withheld this honor from Christopher Columbus, who certainly deserved it, and given it to Amerigo Vespucci, who did not.

Amerigo Vespucci was born in Florence, Italy, in the same year that Columbus was born in Genoa—1451. His first name, Amerigo, is the Ital-

ian form of the German name Emmerrich, which means "rich in wheat." Amerigo grew up to be a business man—a banker for the Florentine house of Medici. As a supplier of ships in the Medici branch in Spain, he was in close touch with many of the men who were just then sailing off to explore parts unknown. Excitement over the New World ran high along the water front, and Vespucci caught the fever. He studied astronomy, geography, and navigation, became expert in all three, and then went to sea.

Just *when* he went, and when he first saw the New World, no one knows. But because the land was named after him, and because many people have thought it should not have been, the question of Amerigo Vespucci's comings and goings has been argued for more than four centuries.

The only proofs are Vespucci's own letters in which he claims to have discovered a continent—a continent which may have been nothing less than North America. There is no other record of the early voyage he claims to have made in 1497—even before Cabot sailed from Bristol.

In 1507, Waldseemüller printed a geography, in which he suggested (in the fifth line at right) that Amerigo Vespucci deserved to have America named after him.

Nūc ẏo & hę partes funt latius luftratæ/& alia quarta pars per Americū Vefputiū(vt in fequentibus audietur)inuenta eft/quā non video cur quis iure vetet ab Americo inuentore fagacis ingenij viro Amerigen quafi Americi terrā/fiue Americam dicendā:cū & Europa & Afia a mulieribus fua fortita fint nomina.Eius fitū & gentis mores ex bis binis Americi nauigationibus quæ fequunt liquide intelligi datur.

Ameri-
ca

On his third voyage to America, in 1498, Columbus found natives fishing for
pearls off the island of Margarita on the coast of Venezuela. After his men
had traded some bits of pottery for three pounds of pearls, they sailed away.
The canoes shown in De Bry's drawing (above) are loaded with pearl oysters.

In 1499, when Ojeda rediscovered Venezuela's pearl fisheries, Columbus was wrongly accused of having held back information about them for his own profit.

Many people have held that Vespucci could not possibly have made the voyage at the time he said he made it.

And yet, there is a strong argument against disbelieving Vespucci. In those famous letters he tells about a coastline which may well have been Florida and territory to the north. He describes the land, the Indians, the animals, and birds, the plants, the climate. And at the same time that he wrote all this *no other explorer had yet visited that shore or even knew it existed.*

But whether or not Vespucci explored North America, there is no doubt that he did make voyage to Brazil. That country had been discovered when the king of Portugal, having sent Vasco de Gama around Africa and eastward to India, decided to set up a trading center in the East. For this purpose he sent out, in the year 1500, a large fleet—thirteen ships and 1,200 men—under command of Pedro Álvarez de Cabral.

But for some reason that has never been explained, Cabral, as soon as he had sailed a few hundred miles down the African route, veered off in the wrong direction. Instead of rounding Africa's Cape of Good Hope and proceeding east, he sailed westward, and a month later reached Brazil in South America.

It may have been a mistake, but this seems unlikely—few navigators of that time knew their business bet-

AMERICVS VESPVCCI

miles, stopping often so that the men could explore the shore.

On New Year's Day they came to what they thought was the mouth of a great river, and because of the date they called it the River of January. It turned out to be a bay, but the city that was built at that place today bear the name Rio de Janeiro.

From Rio they sailed perhaps a thousand miles farther down, to what is now Argentina.

When Amerigo Vespucci returned to Lisbon in 1502 and told the King and his experts about the vast shores he had seen, they began to wonder whether the southern gateway to the commerce of the Orient might be reached by going through and beyond the newly found continent bordering on the southern Atlantic.

The Portuguese thought it made perfectly good sense, therefore, to send Vespucci back the next year to see if he could find his way beyond South America to Malacca, the great seaport on the "Golden Peninsula" of Malaya. This was the purpose of his fourth voyage. But with bad luck and bad management, the venture ended in failure after he reached the Brazilian coast.

Four of the six ships were lost in a storm. Then, after months of investigating the chances of getting through or around Brazil—a country which is bigger than the United

ter than the Portuguese—perhaps he was driven off course by a storm, or, it may have been that Cabral was acting on secret orders. In any case, when he saw land he promptly claimed it for Portugal; and as it lay to the east of the line the Pope had drawn, the claim was undisputed.

The land was the bulge of Brazil. Accordingly, Brazil belonged to Portugal until she proclaimed her independence three centuries later.

A year after Cabral's "accidental" visit to Brazil, Vespucci—now in the employ of the King of Portugal— sailed there with a fleet of three Portuguese caravels on what was to be an important voyage.

From the bulge of Brazil these ships followed down the east coast of South America for many hundreds of

States—Vespucci gave up his quest for the short cut to Malacca and went home. It was as well that he did, considering that in a straight line, Malacca was 14,000 miles away!

Vespucci's letters were printed in Paris, Florence, and many other places. All Europe was hungry for news of the mysterious lands across the Atlantic. The letters were eagerly read. Then, in 1507, they were included in a little 52-page book—*Cosmographiae Introductio*—published in Latin, and written by Martin Waldseemüller. In it he wrote about the geography of three parts of the world, Europe, Asia, and Africa, and then said:

"... and now another fourth part has been discovered by Americus Vespucius, and therefore I see no reason why we should not call it Amerige or America after its discoverer Americus."

And so two continents received a name, and "America" was seen in print for the first time in history.

Vespucci's Spaniards, armed with guns, easily overcame the Indians of Brazil.

Alonso de Ojeda's Spaniards attack an Indian village near present-day Cartagena, Colombia. Ojeda came to America in 1493 with Columbus' second expedition, explored Brazil with Vespucci, and became governor of lands in northern South America in 1508—the year he sailed for Cartagena in an attempt to found a colony there.

THROUGH THE
WALL OF LAND

As the Indians proved bitterly hostile, Ojeda left his men under Francisco Pizarro in 1509, and sailed to Hispaniola hoping to get help for his doomed colony.

On the shore of the Gulf of Darien, where the continent of South America hangs on the thread of Panama, the Indians led Christopher Columbus to the top of a mountain. From that height he could view the country for miles, but not so far as to see the blue of a mighty ocean less than a hundred miles to the west.

It was 1502, and Columbus was completing his fourth and last voyage to the New World.

All through the country, they said, there was gold. They showed him the yellow glint in the sands of a river bottom. They dug up yellow grains from between the roots of a tree, and nine days away, overland to the south, they said, was a great kingdom far richer than their own.

But when he wanted to encamp and explore the land, the Indians forbade him. They were powerful men who carried poisoned arrows and stout bows. Columbus decided to risk going on with the search. The result was three months of bloody warfare and many Spanish dead.

At length, tired, sick, and worried about his rebellious men and his worm-eaten ships, Columbus took one last agonized look at the land which he believed to be the gateway to the long-sought Cathay, and sailed away. On his return to Spain he reported the Indians' stories. Two years later he was dead.

A few years after his death an expedition was organized by a group of settlers on the island of Hispaniola to go to that country and see if the tales of gold were true.

Under the command of Alonso de Ojeda, they tried settling on the shore of what is now Colombia. But they sent word back to Hispaniola that they were starving.

In 1510, Martín Fernández de Enciso, with two supply ships, sailed for Ojeda's colony in Colombia. Hiding on board the ship *Barbara* was a stowaway, a strapping 35-year-old planter of Hispaniola: Vasco Núñez de Balboa.

Like many of his neighbors, Balboa had come to the New World expecting to find gold and go home a rich man. But others had already made off with most of the gold. Balboa had to take to farming. He did so poorly that he could not pay his debts. To escape imprisonment, he stowed away aboard the *Barbara*.

When, after a few days at sea, Balboa came out of hiding, Enciso first threatened to abandon him on a desert island, but finally pardoned him. The ships sailed on to Colombia where they found Ojeda's colony. After taking on board all of Ojeda's party (for Ojeda's desperate colonists had decided to abandon Colombia) Enciso sailed to Darien, on the Isthmus of Panama, to hunt for gold. There, Balboa began planning to get rid of Enciso. Before long he succeeded. Enciso was forcibly put on board a ship and sent home, and Balboa took command.

Balboa wades into the Pacific and claims the lands bordering it for Spain.

On the Isthmus of Panamá, ". . . upon a peak in Darien," Balboa planted a Cross.

In the beginning, the Indians no more welcomed these newcomers than they had those white men who had visited them earlier. Balboa knew how to talk to them. They allowed him to build his town and later they worked for him in the fields and gold mines. In time, Balboa became Governor and Captain General of Darien.

From these natives he learned much about the surrounding country. One day his officers were gathered in his house to divide the gold they had collected from the Indians. As they were weighing it, a violent argument developed.

The Indians could not understand this madness for gold. A young Indian chief stepped up, struck at the scales in disgust, and scattered the gold over the floor.

"If this is what you prize," he said, "I can tell you of a land where the people eat and drink from golden dishes and where gold is as cheap to them as iron is to you."

One man especially was stirred by the Indian's story. His name was Francisco Pizarro.

The country lay far to the south, the Indian said. It could be reached by crossing the land at the narrow place and then going down the shore of the south sea, the great sea, the "Blue Ocean."

As the man spoke, Balboa was in a fever of excitement. The "narrow place!" The "great sea!" A way at last through this vast, bewildering wall of land! And beyond—who could tell? Perhaps Cathay!

Balboa rushed about the town to get together an expedition. He recruited about 190 Spaniards. A few days later, with hundreds of Indians going along as porters and guides, he set out from Darien.

In Balboa's expedition were twelve fierce dogs, for use against the Indians.

The procession advanced along the north shore of the Isthmus of Panama to a point only a few miles from the site of the canal that crosses it today. The Indians had said it was a six-day march to the sea. But they had not mentioned the two ranges of rugged mountains that would have to be scaled; the dank, fever-ridden marshes in the valleys; the jungles; the natives who would swoop down out of the hills, shooting poisoned arrows; the poisonous snakes and the swarming clouds of stinging insects.

As Balboa and his men fought their way southward across the neck of land, the six days stretched to three weeks and their sufferings became all but unbearable.

Their worst enemies were yellow fever and—most horrible of all—ants. No weapon could hold off the murderous swarms of ants. When a man came down with the fever he went mad and began attacking his comrades. Then, for their own safety,

50

they would tie his hands and feet and leave him behind to die. But sometimes, when they had to double back on the trail, they saw what the ants had left of their luckless companions—white skeletons, picked clean in a matter of hours! They decided it would be kinder to kill anyone who fell sick.

It was the morning of September 25, 1513. Only sixty-nine Spaniards were still alive. Balboa called a halt at the base of a hill. He climbed until a new horizon inched up to meet his gaze—the unbroken blue of the Pacific, or as they called it, the *Mar del Zur*—the great South Sea.

Four days later he marched down the beach, into the rolling surf of the Pacific, and still in full armor waded out until he was standing in water waist-deep. There he proclaimed to the wind and waves that he was taking possession for the King of Spain of "all the sea and all the lands bordering upon it."

The King of Spain was not as grateful, however, as might have been expected. Martín Enciso had gone to Spain and reported Balboa's treatment of him to the King.

The story which the angry Indian had told of a "golden kingdom" south of Darien, was also told at the Spanish court. It swept the country. A fleet was made ready with all speed and 1,500 Spanish adventurers embarked for Darien. Enciso was with the expedition which was headed by Pedrarias Dávila (some-times written Pedro Arias de Ávila), a cruel conquistador whom the King appointed, instead of Balboa, to be governor of the new colony. Dávila brutally overworked the Indians so that they died by the thousands. Balboa wrote a letter to the King of Spain, imploring him to put a stop to the cruelty, for which Dávila never forgave him.

Balboa still hoped to reach the golden empire far to the south. It would be safer and easier to cover the distance by sea. He had just completed the work of building two ships when a runner arrived with a letter from Dávila.

The tone of the message was friendly. The Governor, who lived in the new town of Acla, a few miles from Darien, needed some advice from Balboa on certain business matters. Would Balboa come at once to Acla for a conference?

Balboa did as he was asked. On his approach to the town a company of soldiers came marching down the road and arrested him. To his amazement he saw at the head of this company his own trusted lieutenant, Francisco Pizarro.

Balboa asked him why he was being treated in this manner. Pizarro smiled and took him to jail.

Balboa was given a one-day "trial" and Governor Dávila forced the court to sentence him to death. Before the sun set on that autumn day in 1517, in the public square of Acla, Balboa was beheaded.

Mare antiliarum.
SEPTENTRO
Peru
America
Mare aque dulcis
EQVINOCTIALIS
Cambales.
Brasilus.
Quarta orbis pars.
TROPICVS CAPRICORNI
OCCIDENS
Terra argẽtea.
Mundus nouus.
ORIENS
Terra Incognita
Mare muẽti p magalhões.
MERIDIES

THE VAST AND PEACEFUL SEA

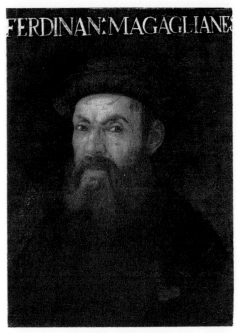

Ferdinand Magellan.

All Europe believed that the nation that could gain control of new seaways to the Orient would probably become the richest on earth. After Columbus' discovery, the leading contenders for this great prize were Spain and Portugal.

The Portuguese had always been secretive about their explorations. Now maps, charts, and reports of explorers came to be closely-guarded state secrets, kept under lock and key in the royal libraries in both Lisbon and Madrid.

Twenty years after Columbus' discovery, a Portuguese naval officer spent many hours eagerly pouring over maps of the New World, the Indies, and the known sailing routes that were kept in the government's chart rooms in Lisbon. His name was Fernando de Magalhaes.

Ferdinand Magellan, as he came to be called in English, was a big sombre man of tremendous strength and iron will. While fighting the Moors in Morocco he was wounded in the leg, which left him with a permanent limp. Now, in his late

A Portuguese map, drawn in 1558, pictures Patagonian Indians just north of the Straits of Magellan, in South America.

thirties, he had come upon the biggest idea of his life.

From the Moluccas, or Spice Islands, came nutmeg, mace, and cloves. Portuguese navigators had only recently found their way there, after Vasco da Gama reached India, in 1498, by sailing around Africa and eastward via the great trading center of Malacca on the Malay Peninsula. In the service of the navy Magellan had been in Malacca. It was a long, dangerous route. Why not, he wondered, try it the other way around—westward across the Atlantic to America, then across the ocean that Balboa had seen? For Magellan felt sure those shores of Panama and the Spice Islands were separated by one body of water.

If he could reach the Spice Islands by sailing westward, then he

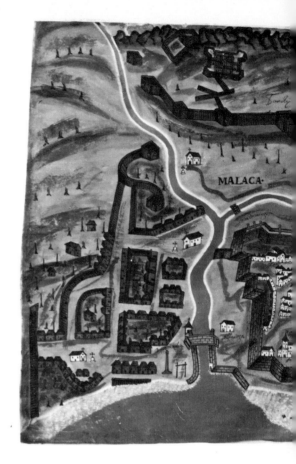

The valuable city of Malacca, on the Malay Peninsula, had belonged to Portugal ever since 1511, when it was captured by Admiral Alonso de Albuquerque.

could continue over the Portuguese route westward to Malacca, westward again to India, from India around Africa, and so on home again to Portugal. In other words, by going west and continuing west, he could *sail around the world!*

There were two flaws in the dream. First, Magellan believed there was a strait, not too hard to reach, which would let him sail right through the American land barrier into Balboa's ocean.

The second was Magellan's guess at the width of the Pacific Ocean. His guess was around 600 miles. The actual distance from the west coast of South America to the Molucca Islands, in a straight line, is more than 11,000 miles!

More immediately, Magellan's blunt honesty had got him into trouble with his superiors in the navy, with whom he often disagreed, and in the ill graces of King Manuel. When he demanded a new commission of the King and was flatly turned down, he decided to leave Portugal forever.

He gathered together a little band of relatives and faithful friends, confided to them his grand scheme to sail around the world, and took them to Spain to see if he could win support there.

In Seville he married the daughter of a rich and powerful government official. This opened the way for him to promote his voyage among the advisers of the young King Charles V. They approved the plan and provided him with five ships and 234 men.

The ships were old and leaky and the men were a shiftless lot who knew nothing about seamanship— mostly tramps and criminals who were in jail and were willing to go for the sake of getting out.

So it was not a very promising beginning. But Magellan put his crews to work at once patching up and rigging the miserable little ships.

54

It took a year to put them in shape, but on September 20, 1519, they sailed, first to the Canary Islands, then south and west to Brazil. In the South Atlantic the frail little vessels were battered mercilessly by storms. Provisions were running low. So was morale.

After a gruelling four-month voyage the ships arrived at the huge mouth of the La Plata River, on the coast of what is now Argentina. Continuing south, three weeks later they had reached that part of the coast where Magellan expected to find the strait. Now the fleet felt its way along, looking into every break in the shoreline. Suddenly on rounding a cape the lookouts shouted that clear water lay due west as far as they could see. Hopefully he set his course westward. But the next day brought shoreline dead ahead and the realization that he had merely sailed into a deep bay.

It was so crushing a blow that he considered turning back. But Magellan made up his mind to go on.

As the cold of winter closed in on them the ships anchored in a harbor. They were at Port St. Julian a bare, windswept haven a thousand miles south of the La Plata River. Here Magellan announced that instead of going home he intended to stay through the winter. The news struck despair into every heart. The three Spanish captains, Gaspar de Quesada, Luis de Mendoza, and Juan de Cartagena, plotted a mutiny. The next day Cartagena led a force of thirty men on board the San Antonio, and took over the ship. At the same time the two other captains went back to their own ships, told their crews of the scheme, and won their support.

For Magellan, the situation was grim indeed. Of the five ships, three were against him. But in striking back he moved even more quickly than had the mutineers. He sent two boats to Mendoza's ship, the Victoria. In the first boat were only five men, led by Magellan's chief police officer, a Portuguese named Espinosa.

Captain Mendoza, thinking Magellan was sending a message of surrender, allowed the five to come aboard the *Victoria*. There followed a brief exchange on deck, and while this was taking place the second boat drew near unnoticed.

Suddenly Espinosa sprang at Mendoza and plunged a dagger into his throat. Before the *Victoria's* men could gather their wits about them, their leader lay dead on the deck and the second boat crew had clambered on board with drawn swords.

When Magellan was 1500 miles east of the Philippines he came upon islands (below) where the natives stole the Victoria's longboat. The crew named them the "Islands of Thieves," or Ladrones. Today they are known as the Marianas.

This rare, old Spanish map was made by Vaz Dourado in 1568. It shows the southernmost tip of South America—with two ships about to enter, and one just leaving the Straits of Magellan. The tree carries the coat of arms of Spain. To the right are four Patagonian Indians.

The stunned sailors immediately surrendered.

This gave Magellan three ships against two, and the rest was easy. That night he sent armed forces against the remaining mutineers, took command of the ships, and arrested the ringleaders. In one day he had put down the mutiny and had his enemies at his mercy. All the sailors were pardoned; but as an example to anyone who might get

On Mactan Island (below) near Cebu in the Philippines, Magellan was killed by natives. The two small pictures here come from the diary of Antonio Pigafetta, —Magellan's young Italian secretary— one of the few crewmen to reach home.

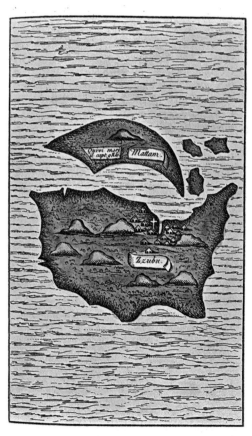

They were much larger than Magellan's Spaniards—so large that the crews called them "patagón," the Spanish word for "beast-footed." They dressed in tapir skins, and were the most primitive men the Spaniards had ever seen. One was captured and died aboard the Victoria.

57

This 16th century drawing of Magellan's Victoria, *is framed with a Latin inscription, part of which reads "My sails are wings, glory my reward."*

such ideas in the future, Captain Quesada was beheaded.

Wintertime that far south comes in the months of June, July, and August. The ice in the harbor had barely begun to melt toward the end of August when Magellan ordered anchors up, and the fleet resumed its weary way southward. One ship, the *Santiago*, had been wrecked during the winter, so now there were four.

On leaving Port St. Julian, Magellan inflicted a terrible punishment on Cartagena and his assistant in the mutiny. Still in bitter cold, the two men were taken ashore in that remote and desolate part of the world and left there. Of course, the men were never heard from again.

Violent headwinds, the tag end of winter, still made for rough sailing southward down the coast. On October 21, 1520, the fleet rounded a headland and finding a wide bay, made into it. It looked nearly land-locked, but two ships continued westward, and found an opening on the other side which allowed the fleet to hold its course. This proved the beginning of the long-sought channel joining two oceans, called the Straits of Magellan.

Through the twisting passage, wide in some places, in others closing to half a mile between tall cliffs, the ships threaded their way for 375 miles. Only the greatest of sailors could have brought even a small vessel safely through those hazardous gorges.

No human beings were seen, but at night the cliffs were dotted with flame. These fires were kept by natives who had not changed their ways since the Stone Age. Never having learned how to kindle a flame, each one had to keep his own campfire burning all the time. The Spaniards named the land Tierra del Fuego, land of fire.

It took Magellan more than five weeks to pick his way through the strait. At last, approaching the coast of Chile, he saw before him the great ocean. At the sight, the crew, confident now of a quick crossing to the Moluccas, of making a fortune at last, burst into wild cheers. But Magellan did not join them. For sheer joy and gratitude, the man of iron was weeping.

Meanwhile one of the ships, the *San Antonio*, was lagging behind. Her pilot, another cousin of Magellan named Estevao Gómez, had lost his nerve and was stirring up a new plot among his shipmates to escape. On the very day that the advance ships saw the ocean beyond, this gang overpowered their captain, wore the ship about, and sailed back through the strait to the Atlantic side, bound for Spain.

In 1586, a German book of navigation carried this map of Magellan's Straits.

The missing vessel, largest of the four, was carrying most of the provisions. Now the possibility of running out of food in mid-ocean terrified even the most loyal of the men, and all wanted to turn back.

Not so Magellan. They would go on to the Moluccas, he said, if they had to eat the leather off the ships' yards! And go they did.. After a month on the inhospitable Chilean shore, the three remaining ships set sail, first to the north to get out of the cold, then westward on the great ocean.

With a fine following breeze and gentle water, the going now was smooth and fast. This ocean was so calm that the men began calling it *El Pacifico*—The Peaceful Sea.

They lost their fondness for it as the days rolled on into weeks and the

This map—bordered with gold—was once owned by Emperor Charles V of Spain.

It traces Magellan's world voyage and was made around 1545 by Battista Agnese.

61

INSVLA MATHAN.

Victoria

Here the natives of Mactan, in the Philippines, are shown attacking Magellan.

in a diary kept by one of the sailors: "We were forced to eat the crumbs and powder that was left of our bread, being now full of worms. Our drinking water was putrified and yellow. We ate the pieces of leather that were wrapped around the yards of the ships.

"By reason of this famine and unclean eating, our gums began to swell and grow over our teeth [one of the symptoms of scurvy] and many of us sickened and some died."

At last, nearly four months after he had set sail from South America, Magellan found land worth visiting —a group of islands, distant outposts of the Orient. Here were dates, bananas, coconuts, and other fresh fruits and meats. Their scurvy would be cured.

Natives swarmed aboard the ships. They were friendly enough, but because they stole everything they could lay hands on, Magellan named the islands the Ladrones—Islands of Thieves—part of the group known today as the Marianas.

He paused only long enough to take on supplies, then resumed his way westward in hopes of soon reaching the Moluccas. A week later he thought he had reached his goal, but the shore he saw was an island of the group that was later named the Philippines.

weeks into months of vainly scanning this incredible waste of water. Before they saw any land at all, they had sailed nearly twice as long as Columbus had in crossing the Atlantic, and then found only a tiny islet of no help or comfort to them.

Still ahead lay more thousands of miles. And now under the oppressive heat, starvation beset them, and disease, and death. Magellan had to fulfill the vow he had made in a moment of bravado—that if necessary he would eat the leather that was wrapped around the yards of the ship. The story of this ordeal is told

Although Magellan was the first European to visit these islands, he met traders from China and other parts of the Far East, and from them he learned that he could reach the Moluccas by sailing a few hundred miles to the south.

It was Magellan's great moment of triumph and also of awe—triumph because he knew he could reach the Moluccas and from those islands continue over the familiar route back to Spain, thus demonstrating that the earth was round by sailing around it; and awe at the sheer size of the globe, so much greater than Europeans had dreamed it was!

But for poor Magellan it was a very brief triumph indeed. Shortly after his arrival at the Philippines he tried to protect one group of natives, whom he had befriended, against an enemy tribe. Leading fifty of his men through a jungle, he found himself surrounded by a great mob of hundreds of angry warriors. The little group of Spaniards was put to rout. But Magellan, hampered by his game leg, was overtaken and done to death by the spears of the savages.

After this defeat, even the "friendly" natives turned on the white men and massacred many more. Now there were not enough left to work three ships, so they burned one, and in the flagships *Trinidad* and the *Victoria*, fled from the Philippines.

More weeks of hardships and

Juan Sebastian del Cano sailed the Victoria *home to Spain, after Magellan's death.*

He reached Sanlúcar, Spain, with 18 survivors on September 7, 1522. Emperor Charles V awarded him, and not Magellan, the coat of arms (left). Wrapped around the globe is the Latin inscription: Primus circumdedisti me! ("You were first to sail around me!")

death brought them at last to the Moluccas. There they loaded up with spices. So eager were the sailors to make the most of this business that they even took off their shirts and trousers and traded them for these precious commodities!

By this time, of the 234 men who had sailed from Spain, only 101 remained alive. While 47 embarked in the *Victoria* for the long voyage westward across the Indian Ocean and down around Africa, bound for Spain, the *Trinidad* was so leaky she had to stay behind for repairs.

The *Victoria*, after a long siege of starvation and scurvy which took many more lives, at last, with only eighteen haggard survivors, reached Spain in 1522—the first ship ever to sail around the world.

THE ISLAND
OF FLORIDA

Many an adventurer reached North America within a few years after Columbus' discovery. Among them, the first to be authentically identified as a visitor to the part of the continent that is now the United States was a Spanish soldier named Juan Ponce de León.

Ponce de León sailed with Columbus on his second voyage to America in 1493. At the Spanish settlement in Hispaniola he served in the force that subjugated and enslaved the Indians of that island. Then he explored and conquered Puerto Rico, in 1509, where he established a large estate for himself, built a castle, and ruled as governor.

In the gold mines and plantations of Hispaniola the Indians were dying off so fast from undernourishment and overwork that their masters had to keep sending to nearby islands for replacements. From these islanders they heard tales of a fabulous land— the Indians described it incorrectly as an island—not far away to the north, which they called Bimini.

Though the shape of Florida is not accurate here, it is shown as a peninsula in this map drawn by Le Moyne in 1564. Half a century earlier, in 1513, Ponce de León believed Florida was an island.

For years, Ponce de León had heard talk of Bimini. He wanted the honors and riches that would go to the first men to find it for Spain. An added attraction was a tale told to him by an imaginative old Indian woman. In Bimini, she said, a magic fountain flowed eternally. Old and middle-aged people, on drinking its waters, would become young again. The greying conquistador, then in his fifties, listened with deep interest.

In the spring of 1513 he set sail from Puerto Rico with three caravels. His course to the northwest lay through the whole chain of the Bahamas, more than 700 islands, keys,

small bits of rock and reef. He could not explore them all, but he did visit several islands, including San Salvador, where Columbus had made his first landfall in the new world.

On Easter Sunday, March 27, 1513, Ponce de León got his first look at the coast of what is now the United States. He was near the spot where, 52 years later, the town of St. Augustine was to be founded, the oldest town that still exists in the United States.

Because of the day when he first beheld the land, Ponce de León called it *Florida*, for "Pascua de

The Gulf of Mexico was sketched in 1520, a year after Piñeda's voyage. Florida is labeled "the land they call Bimini, discovered by Juan Ponce de León." The map proves Piñeda, and not de Soto, discovered the Mississippi—for the river's mouth appears, labeled Río del Espíritu santo (*River of the Holy Ghost.*)

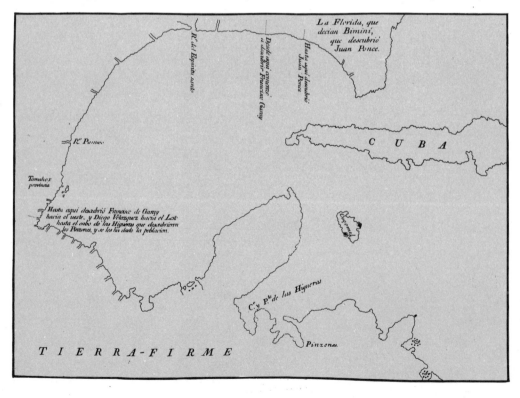

In Florida, Ponce de León's men used guns and dogs against hostile Indians.

Flores," the Spanish name for Easter
—the time of year that brings the
first flowers. Six days later, when he
found a safe spot to make a landing,
he went ashore, raised the royal ban-
ner, and claimed possession of the
country for Spain.

The Indians of this country, he
quickly learned, were not like the
timid, defenseless people who had
been so easily subdued in Hispaniola.
These men were fierce fighters.
Though they had no weapons to
match the white men's guns, they
had bows and arrows tipped with
poison. Above all, they had spirit.
They were ready to fight.

Ponce de León and his followers
ventured to land only a few times
and never once did they dare to explore the interior.

The fleet turned south and went
down along the east coast to Cape
Canaveral, where today rockets are
sent into outer space in a new kind
of exploration. On rounding the cape
they encountered the full force of the

Juan Ponce de León.

Of Florida.

A Florida Indian woman. The pictures on this page were painted in 1585— about 75 years after Ponce de León's visit.

it as "the Island of Florida." He had not found the Fountain of Youth, but then, he really had not given himself much opportunity to look for it. He would like to go back, better equipped. The King promised him that if he could conquer Florida he could be its governor.

For the next few years Ponce de León was kept busy putting down revolts of the Carib tribe in the West Indies. But in 1521 he set out for Florida again, this time with two well-armed ships and 200 trained fighting men and 50 horses. He intended to set up a permanent colony. He had invested his entire fortune in the expedition.

When he reached Florida he led ashore the crew of one of the vessels, but immediately he was met by an overwhelming force of furious Indians. Although the white men were clad in armor, so powerful were the great bows of these natives that they could crack a helmet or drive an arrow through the chain mail of the Spaniards.

The Indians killed and wounded many of the invaders and made short work of driving them off. One of the arrows pierced Ponce de León's armor and went into his thigh. He fell to the beach. His companions picked him up and carried him back to the ship. There was no doctor

Gulf Stream. Struggling for weeks against this mighty current, they picked their way along the Florida Keys, then followed up the west coast until it took a sharp bend to the westward. Then they turned back for home.

Ponce de León did not know whether the land he had seen was an island or not, but he knew for certain that it was very large—even bigger than the great island of Cuba —and he considered his discovery so important that he went to Spain to tell the King about it. He spoke of

This tattooed Florida warrior carries a quiver full of poisoned arrows and a powerful bow more than six feet long.

among the company. Hoping to find one in Havana, Cuba, they set sail at once. But a few days after he was brought to that town, Ponce de León died of his wound.

Although Ponce de León never learned whether it was an island or a continent that he had found, other Spanish voyagers had visited Florida before he made his second trip and had proved it was part of the great American mainland.

The most interesting of these ventures was headed by Alonzo Alvarez de Piñeda in 1519. At the same time that Magellan was looking for a strait into the Pacific thousands of miles to the south, Piñeda sailed from the island of Jamaica to Florida with the same purpose in mind.

For nine months his fleet of four caravels combed the long shore of the Gulf of Mexico, up the west side of Florida, then around to where the city of Tampico is located. Finding no opening into the "South Sea," he turned back.

On his way eastward Piñeda came upon a "river of great waters" which he named *Río del Espíritu Santo,* or River of the Holy Ghost. Although Hernando de Soto is generally given credit for the discovery

of the Mississippi, it is practically certain that it was this river which Piñeda reached more than twenty years before de Soto.

In the Florida swamps Ponce de León encountered alligators as well as Indians.

THE CONQUEST OF MEXICO AND PERU

Ship after ship, crowded with fortune hunters, sailed in the wake of Columbus to the New World. Many lost their lives in the gamble, many went home empty-handed. A few grew rich from gold mines and pearl fisheries. Others prospered by working the land with slave labor. And from Mexico and Peru the conquistadors took huge treasures.

Robbery and oppression met with less protest in those times than today. Violence and cruelty were common —in the "civilized" world of Europe as well as among the "savage" peoples of America. The crime of aggression was called "conquest." Mass murder sometimes became a necessary part of conquest. White men who needed to justify themselves often charged the Indians with eating human flesh, and said that the Indians did not worship the true God. Sometimes the Indians said the same of their tormentors. The white men, having superior tools for murder—steel weapons, gunpowder, and guns—could do more killing than the savages.

Bartolomé de Las Casas, a Spanish priest, came to America in 1502 and spent many years in the new settlements. He charged his fellow-Span-

Hernando Cortés landed at Vera Cruz in April, 1519. He burnt his eleven ships in August—so that his soldiers could not retreat—and marched on Mexico City.

iards with the killing of huge numbers of Indians. Other historians, writing hundreds of years later, have accused him of exaggerating. But those historians were not there; Las Casas was. "I saw with my own eyes," he wrote, "above six thousand children die in three or four months."

But the Spanish were too absorbed in their quest for gold to heed Las Casas. From the western tip of Cuba the coast of Yucatán lies only a little more than a hundred miles across the Caribbean. Spanish raiders tried one of their invasions there but were driven off by defiant Maya Indians. On their return to Cuba they reported that they had seen the natives wearing gold.

The story excited Governor Velásquez of Cuba. At once he organized an expedition of four ships and in 1518 sent them to Yucatán with his nephew, Juan de Grijalva.

There the Maya Indians fought fiercely. But they had never learned the use of iron, and without that metal and without guns they were at a terrible disadvantage. Their only armor was made of quilted cotton and the only cutting edge they had on their arrows, spears, and swords consisted of sharpened chips of obsidian, a brittle volcanic glass. In a pitched battle they lost several hundred men, then turned and fled.

Word spread quickly of the terrible powers of the Spaniards. They were left free to explore the country without further resistance from the natives. They coasted a few hundred miles, until they reached the site of the present city of Veracruz, Mexico. Here they were only 400 miles from the great Aztec capital, Tenochtitlán (Mexico City).

Grijalva saw enough to convince him that he was skirting the fringes of a vast empire, far richer than any country yet seen in the new world.

He saw large stone houses and magnificent temples. From the people he talked with, Grijalva learned that the ruler of the Aztec Empire owned huge quantities of gold which he stored away in great warehouses.

Grijalva also learned that the empire was taking so much from its people in taxes that many cities were on the verge of revolt. Grijalva hurried back to Cuba to tell the news to his uncle, the governor.

Governor Velásquez at once began

Diego de Velásquez (below) Governor of Cuba, chose Cortés to command the Mexican expedition.

Bartolomé de Las Casas (above) tried to stop the Spanish from enslaving Caribbean Indians.

Juan de Grijalva (below) was the first Spaniard to learn of Montezuma's Mexican cities of gold.

In the temples of Mexico, Aztec priests led human victims up the steps to the altars, and sacrificed them to the sun. When Cortés reached Tenochtitlán (Mexico City) he found the temple there decorated with 136,000 human skulls.

getting together a heavily-armed "exploring party." But Grijalva, to his surprise and chagrin, was not chosen to lead this expedition. A 34-year-old soldier-politician named Hernando Cortés had plotted against Grijalva, and neatly turned Governor Velásquez against his own nephew. So it was Cortés who won the invasion of Mexico. With eleven ships and 600 men, he set off in February, 1519, to see what he could gain for Spain—and for himself—from the mighty empire that lay behind the coast.

Cortés landed in Mexico on Good Friday, April 22, 1519. He had been warned that his 700 men would have to face huge armies of disciplined troops numbering in the tens of thousands. But he knew, too, that his tiny band of invaders carried war-making equipment which the Indians could not match—armor that would turn their arrows, deadly crossbows, guns, and roaring cannons that would strike terror into the heart of the bravest barbarian.

Also, he took along sixteen horses. As there were no horses in America

In this 16th century drawing, a priest with an obsidian knife offers the heart of his victim to Tonatiuh, the sun god.

before the Spaniards brought them over, the Indians were amazed and terribly frightened when Cortés' mounted soldiers came charging into battle against them at Tabasco—the horses' hooves beating the earth, harnesses jingling, and the men brandishing steel. The Aztecs thought men and horse were one creature!

The situation in Mexico was even luckier for Hernando Cortés and the Spanish than Grijalva had suggested. Long ago, the people of Mexico believed, a god named Quetzalcoatl came across the water from the east to their land with several companion gods. They had white faces and wore beards. For a time they ruled over the people of Mexico, and they proved gentle and kind and good. Then the people turned against them and drove them away. But as Quetzalcoatl departed he said that some day he would return and punish the whole country for its wickedness.

Everyone in Mexico, the priests, even the emperor—the mighty Montezuma himself—believed this story which had come down to them from their ancestors. Hence when Cortés and his marauders appeared on the scene, the Aztecs were sure the day of judgment had arrived and the white gods had returned to wreak their vengeance.

As he had hoped, Cortés was able

Montezuma's envoys greet Cortés, on his march to Mexico City. In the background the volcano, Popocatepetl, is erupting.

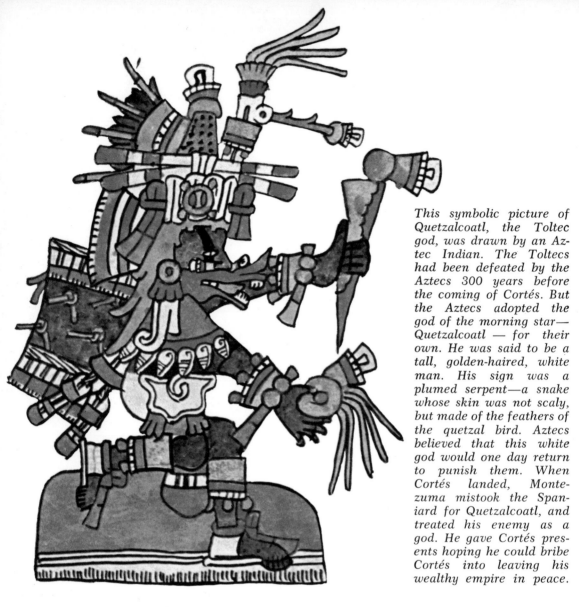

This symbolic picture of Quetzalcoatl, the Toltec god, was drawn by an Aztec Indian. The Toltecs had been defeated by the Aztecs 300 years before the coming of Cortés. But the Aztecs adopted the god of the morning star— Quetzalcoatl — for their own. He was said to be a tall, golden-haired, white man. His sign was a plumed serpent—a snake whose skin was not scaly, but made of the feathers of the quetzal bird. Aztecs believed that this white god would one day return to punish them. When Cortés landed, Montezuma mistook the Spaniard for Quetzalcoatl, and treated his enemy as a god. He gave Cortés presents hoping he could bribe Cortés into leaving his wealthy empire in peace.

Samples of gold jewelry made by the Aztecs (below) include the head of a god, an owl, a monkey, and a serpent. Pieces like these, carried back to Europe in treasure galleons by the Spanish, are now preserved in the world's art museums.

This 16th century watercolor shows Cortés' army, followed by Indian porters, marching on Mexico City. At far right, next to Cortés, stands Malintzin Tenepal, the Indian girl Cortés called Doña Marina, and who became his interpreter.

in a short time to win great parts of the Aztec empire over to his side by promising to free them from the tyrannical rule of Montezuma. Soon he was leading thousands of Indian troops against the Mexican capital, Tenochtitlán.

He marched into the city, pretended friendship for Montezuma, and then treacherously seized him and held him as prisoner and hostage.

The people of Mexico were hopelessly confused. Their mighty ruler,

When Cortés first saw Mexico City, it was surrounded by an artificial lake and connected to the shore by causeways. The lake was dotted with chinampas, or flowery islets called "floating gardens."

75

This copy of an Aztec Indian drawing shows Montezuma (seated with Cortés) discussing his ransom. Doña Marina stands at right. The original of this sketch was made shortly after Montezuma was taken prisoner on November 14, 1519.

their "angry lord," Montezuma, remained in the hands of the Spanish invaders and they did not want to see him hurt. In fact, he himself kept insisting that these white men were gods and sent messages out to his people urging them not to fight, although the Spanish were killing the Indians by the thousands, in battle after battle.

But there were other men among the Aztecs, princes and powerful leaders of the army, who were not as easily deceived as Montezuma. In time they realized these invaders

In 1521, Cortés beseiged the capital of the Aztecs. Here his gunboats are shown battering down the city walls.

were not gods returning to mete out righteous punishment but only men who had come to rob them and destroy the empire.

These men rose up and led the people of Mexico against the Spaniards. As throngs gathered menacingly around the palace where Montezuma was held prisoner, Cortés prevailed upon him to go out on the roof and speak to the people, begging them not to attack. But now the furious crowds had lost respect for their own emperor. They stoned Montezuma until he fell, fatally injured.

Then on June 30, 1520, the Indian armies closed in on the Spaniards. In a night of fierce battle—called the *Noche Triste*, or "the Night of Sorrow"—many Spaniards were killed and others, fighting their way out of the city, barely escaped across the causeways with their lives.

From a safe distance Cortés built up his army again, then once more marched on the capital. This time he laid siege to it. With thousands of Indian rebels to help him, he kept the city surrounded and cut off from supplies for three months. Finally the Aztec defenders, weakened by slaughter and starvation, were forced to surrender. On August 13, 1521, Cortés marched in triumphantly and the conquest of Mexico was com-

For 75 days after the fighting began on August 13, Indian warriors defended the city, only to lose to Cortés.

plete. After that the country was called New Spain. Other Spaniards came in, Cortés rebuilt the capital, and he and his successors ruled over the land from that time on.

In much the same manner Francisco Pizarro marched on the ancient empire of the Incas in Peru a few years later.

Ever since that day in Darien when he had heard an Indian tell Núñez Balboa about the great golden kingdom of "Birú" that lay to the south, Pizarro had dreamed of making this conquest. Twice he organized expeditions and both times failed. In 1531 he set sail southward from Panamá with three ships in another attempt.

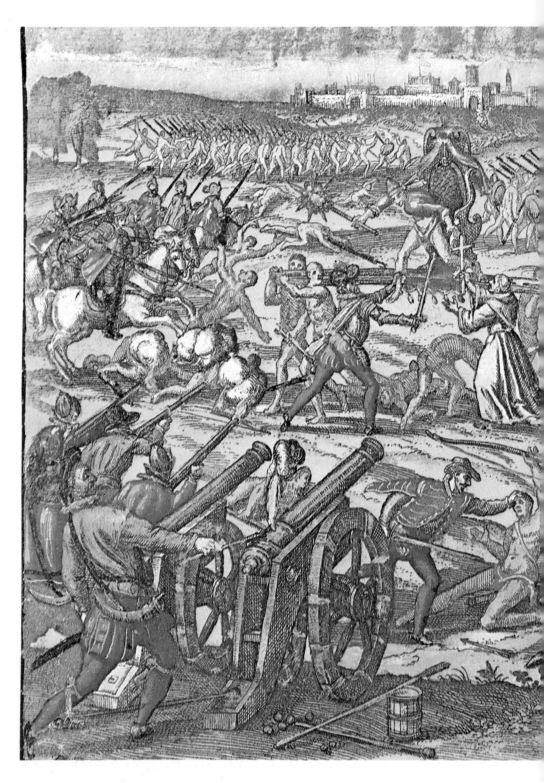

At Cajamarca, Atahualpa was carried to the Spaniards on a golden throne. But when Friar Valverde, Pizarro's chaplain, tried to convert him to Catholicism, the Inca emperor seized Valverde's Bible, in a rage, and flung it to earth.

"Set on, at once; I absolve you," said
Valverde. And with that Pizarro's men
came out of hiding and began to fight.

Like the Aztecs in Mexico, the Incas of Peru were torn and weakened by internal strife, and again the Spaniards were able to take advantage of their unlucky situation. Pizarro, with 180 soldiers, including 27 horsemen, marched into the country, easily won a few skirmishes with the first Indians he met, and made his way through the high mountain passes of the Andes to the town of Cajamarca. This was the home of the emperor, **Atahualpa**.

Here, as boldly as Cortés had entered Mexico, Pizarro marched into the town and camped his army in the large central square. Atahualpa made no attempt to keep the Spaniards out because he was confident he had the Spaniards trapped.

Pizarro sent word to Atahualpa, inviting him to come into the camp for negotiations. Atahualpa accepted the invitation. Next day November 16, 1532, he was carried into Pizarro's camp on a litter, bringing with him 4,000 men, his courtiers, his high prests, his army leaders, and numerous guards.

Pizarro meanwhile had concealed himself and his men behind walls and buildings around the plaza. As the Inca dignitaries moved to the center of the square they found only a Spanish priest carrying a Bible and an Indian interpreter. The priest told Atahualpa and his followers they must surrender to Spain and give up their worship of false gods for the religion of the Spaniards.

slashing them with their steel blades. Atahualpa was seized by Pizarro's men and carried off.

In half an hour it was over. The plaza was heaped with the bodies of the 4,000 men, the entire leadership of the great Inca empire.

After that, the conquest of Peru was a simple matter. When it was finished, one of the greatest orgies of plunder of all times began. Marauding bands of Spaniards went through the country, destroying temples, making off with gold ornaments and vessels. The stunned people of Peru, without a government, without commanders for their armies, offered no opposition. In November, 1533, the Spaniards took over the capital city of Cuzco.

Pizarro had a talk with Atahualpa. He offered to release the emperor if the people would gather up and bring in a ransom in gold big enough to satisfy him.

Atahualpa stood against the wall of the room where he was being held prisoner. The room was 22 feet long and 17 feet wide—the size of a large living room in a house of modern times. He reached as high as he could and made a mark on the wall. For his freedom, he would ask his people to fill the room with gold up to that mark.

Atahualpa became enraged. He said he wished to see the prayerbook the priest was carrying. On being handed it, he flung the Bible to the ground.

At that moment Pizarro sprang from his hiding place, shouting *"Santiago!"* ("St. James!")—the battle cry of the Spaniards. This was the signal for his men to attack.

They dashed in, surrounding the Indian leaders who were crowded together in the middle of the square. The guns blazed out. The cannons roared. Those who were not killed outright gaped in astonishment as the horsemen charged straight into them, trampling them underfoot and

A Spanish soldier stands guard over the Inca Atahualpa, who sits chained hand and foot in his prison, waiting for his enormous ransom in gold to be raised.

Pizarro agreed and the treasure began pouring in. It is impossible to state its exact value in terms of today's money, but a fair estimate would put the amount well over $100,000,000.

The room was not filled with gold up to Atahualpa's mark, but this was because the Spaniards themselves were making it impossible by removing some of the gold and storing it elsewhere. Atahualpa demanded that Pizarro set him free.

Pizarro instead accused Atahualpa of secretly sending out messages to Inca warriors who were encamped two days away from Cajamarca, urging them to revolt.

The Spaniards put Atahualpa on trial for his life. Pizarro promptly found him guilty and sentenced him to be burned at the stake. The Inca emperor appealed for mercy. Pizarro then told him that if he would consent to be baptized as a Christian, he would not be burned, and indeed not one drop of his blood would be shed.

Atahualpa consented. A Spanish priest was brought in and the rite of baptism was performed. Immediately afterward, Pizarro's men took Atahualpa out to the middle of the public square in Cajamarca. Instead of burning him or shedding his blood, they strangled him to death.

In 1531, Francisco Pizarro and 180 men set off for "Birú" (Peru). By November 1532, he had imprisoned Inca Atahualpa and had become master of the country.

Before the coming of the Spaniards, the Indians had never known horses or guns. Without them, Spain could never have terrorized Mexico and Peru. The horse, at left, in this Mexican Indian picture-calendar of the 1520's, shows how surprised men of the New World must have been to see the strange, new creature.

VERRAZANO'S ORIENTAL SEA

While Cortés was conquering Mexico for Spain, the little Spanish caravel *Victoria*, in a distant part of the world, was seeking a greater prize. From the day in September, 1522, when this lone survivor of Magellan's fleet limped home to a Spanish port—having circumnavigated the globe—the rivalry among nations for a westward route to the Indies grew fierce.

The *Victoria*, though it had taken two years, had proved that it was possible to sail westward to the Spice Islands. Now, if an easier shorter way could be found through the American land barrier—a strait farther north than the one Magellan had discovered—geographers believed European ships could reach the Spice Islands in 100 days.

To the two leading competitors, Spain and Portugal, a third was added. The *Victoria*'s triumph was not the kind of news that could be kept secret. Five months later, King

Francis I of France was rushing preparations for a voyage to find the short route to the Indies. To head the expedition he chose a member of a great Italian family with important banking connections in France, a skillful navigator named Giovanni da Verrazano.

The King provided four ships. After delays by storms and other troubles that deprived him of three of his vessels, Verrazano sailed secretly from an uninhabited islet near Madeira in January, 1524, in his one remaining ship, the *Dauphine*. She carried a crew of 50 and provisions for eight months. Seven weeks later Verrazano sighted "a new land, never before seen by anyone, ancient or modern," as he described it afterwards in a letter to King Francis.

What he saw was the Carolina coast, south of Cape Fear. "My intention," he wrote, "was to reach Cathay, and I had not expected to find such an obstacle of new land. I thought it to be not without some strait to penetrate to the Eastern Ocean."

Looking for the "strait" he coasted southward 200 miles. But here, afraid he might be approaching the territory of the Spanish, he turned back. The men went ashore and met a crowd of Indians, who brought food. Later, from an anchorage in a bay, Verrazano saw great fires lighting up the coast, which he took to be signs of large towns. Heavy surf made a landing dangerous, but next morning a sailor volunteered to swim ashore. Hoping to trade with the Indians, he strapped a bag of trinkets to his back.

The water was rougher than he expected. He nearly drowned. When a wave hurled him up on the beach, he lay there exhausted. Some Indians ran to him. Screaming in terror, he was dragged to a fire and stripped of his clothes. The people

Giovanni da Verrazano, a Florentine in the employ of Francis I of France, explored the coast of North America, in 1524, in his ship, the Dauphine. *He was the first European known to have discovered New York Bay and the Hudson River.*

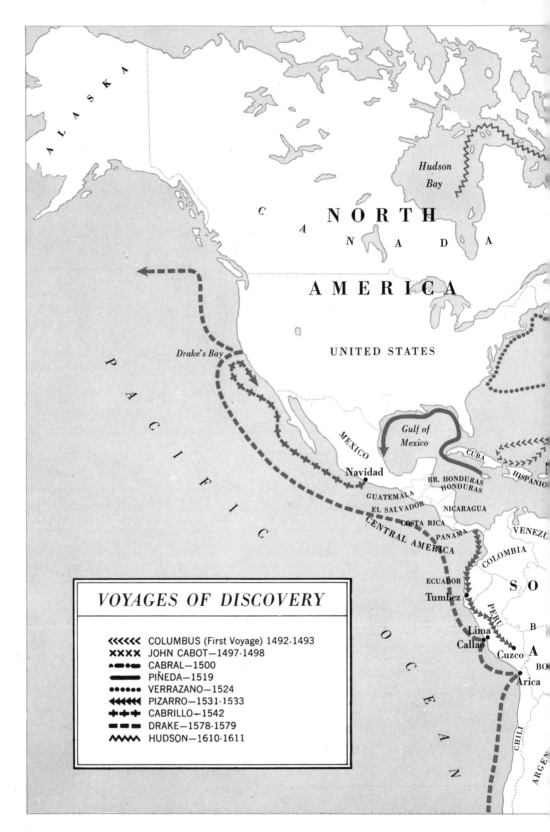

VOYAGES OF DISCOVERY

〈〈〈〈〈	COLUMBUS (First Voyage) 1492-1493
✕✕✕✕	JOHN CABOT—1497-1498
▲●▬●●	CABRAL—1500
▬▬▬	PIÑEDA—1519
●●●●●	VERRAZANO—1524
◄◄◄◄◄	PIZARRO—1531-1533
✛✛✛	CABRILLO—1542
▬ ▬ ▬	DRAKE—1578-1579
∿∿∿	HUDSON—1610-1611

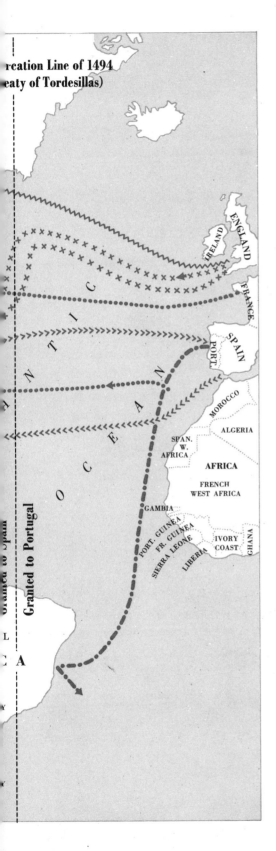

rcation Line of 1494
eaty of Tordesillas)

Granted to Portugal

ENGLAND
IRELAND
FRANCE
SPAIN
PORT.
MOROCCO
ALGERIA
SPAN. W. AFRICA
AFRICA
FRENCH WEST AFRICA
GAMBIA
PORT. GUINEA
FR. GUINEA
SIERRA LEONE
LIBERIA
IVORY COAST
GHANA
ATLANTIC OCEAN

watching from the *Dauphine* were sure their shipmate was about to be roasted and eaten. But the Indians "performed great acts of admiration, regarding the whiteness of his flesh, examining him from head to foot," and when he revived, let him go.

Proceeding north and east, Verrazano sailed past along the Carolina outer Banks. He described the Banks as "an isthmus, a mile across and about 200 miles long, beyond which, from the ship, could be seen the Oriental Sea." Actually this was Pamlico Sound, which separates Hatteras from the North Carolina mainland. "This is the sea, no doubt," Verrazano blithely added, "that borders on the extremity of India and Cathay. We navigated along the isthmus, ever in hopes of finding some strait or true promontory at which the land would end, in order to be able to penetrate to those blessed shores of Cathay."

Farther up the coast, off Virginia or Maryland, the Frenchmen went ashore again. Here in a shabby return for the kindnesses shown them by the Indians, they kidnapped a little boy. Why they did this cruel thing is not explained. Exploring the land again in the vicinity of Delaware, they saw an Indian coming toward them with a burning stick in his hand. Fire was an essential and, for the Indians, very difficult to get started. To offer it to a stranger was a sign of hospitality.

At length they reached a "very agreeable situation" where a great river met the sea. Verrazano anchored again and sent a boat through a narrow channel between two hills. Inside was a bay, where many canoes were passing back and forth.

The Frenchmen considered it one of the finest harbors in the world, and they were right. A century later a town was started by Europeans at that place, and largely because of the harbor, it grew into a great city. How astonished Verrazano and his little band would have been if, as they gazed at that wild shore, by some magic the calendar could have been turned ahead and they could have beheld the scene four centuries later—giant ocean liners docking in that same harbor, in the shadow of the skyscrapers of New York.

As the weather was threatening, the men hurried back to their ship, and Verrazano resumed his coasting. He saw Block Island and Cape Cod and stopped in the harbor of Newport, Rhode Island. The natives were friendly and burning with curiosity about everything that belonged to the white men. Verrazano was enthralled by the land and the people, and spent two weeks there. Then the *Dauphine* continued on her way "down East," passing 32 islands off the coast of Maine, and far beyond until she reached the great cod fishery on the Grand Banks of Newfoundland. From there Verrazano set his course out to sea, homeward bound. He arrived back in Dieppe, France, early in July.

By mistaking Pamlico Sound for the "Oriental Sea" that "no doubt" washed the shores of China—an error quite understandable at the time he lived—Verrazano added to Europe's confusion concerning America. His voyage, nevertheless, was of immense importance in other ways. He could claim the discovery of more than 2,000 miles of the North American coastline. From him the geographers might have learned that the distance between South Carolina and Newfoundland was not filled with sea and islands, as had been supposed, but by an extension of the unbroken shore of a continent.

However, in those days, geographical knowledge did not pass freely from country to country. France kept secrets from Spain, and Spain hid what her mariners discovered from Portugal. And so, other explorers continued to look for the straits which Verrazano had failed to find.

In 1525, Estevao Gómez sailed from Newfoundland to Florida, looking for a passage to the Indies for Charles V of Spain. And in 1536, Sebastian Cabot still did not know whether or not it was one or several continents which stretched from the Mississippi River to Newfoundland.

So Verrazano's voyage did not prove that there was no passage through the New World to the Indies, even though he had sailed up the east coast of North America, and had probably been the first European to discover New York Bay.

In Virginia, Verrazano's sailor probably met Indians like these.

The first white man ever to see buffalo on the Plains of North America was probably Cabeza de Vaca. Other Europeans soon learned of the huge, shaggy beast through pictures like this one, which was made in 1558.

FIRST ACROSS THE LAND

When Spaniards talked of finding another treasure trove like the one Cortés had recently chanced upon in Mexico, they often mentioned the mysterious land that Ponce de León had named Florida. Among those who listened to the persistent buzz about gold was Pánfilo de Narváez. Twenty years earlier he had served as a captain in the subjugation of Cuba. Now back in Spain, and approaching fifty, he reminisced with pride on his prowess as an Indian fighter. He would like to conquer that land to the north of Mexico. He was warned that it would not be easy. The Indians were deadly archers. But he only smiled. Bows and arrows were not guns.

In 1528 Narváez led a fleet and a force of 400 men on an expedition to Florida. But the venture turned out to be a complete disaster.

After he had gone ashore on the west side of Florida near the site of Tampa, Narváez lost his ships. Then, in a long inland march to the north and west, he failed to find gold such as had been found in Mexico. In the wilderness the men went through incredible suffering.

Months of starvation, disease, and Indian attacks reduced their number to 240. One wrote afterwards: "The best armor we had was of no use. Many a coat of chain mail was pierced through and through by the arrows of the Indians. Some of our men swore they had seen a single arrow go through two young oak trees growing close together, each as thick as a man's leg. I myself have seen one of those arrows bury itself a good six inches in a poplar stump. The Indians were marvelously built —lean, strong and agile. Their bows were as thick as a man's arm. And they could shoot with such perfect aim that they never missed, even at two hundred paces."

Spanish halberds, or battle-axes, were mounted on poles five to seven feet long.

At length, in a desperate effort to get back to civilization, the Spaniards built five boats out of what they could find. The plan was to follow the coast around the Gulf, down to Pánuco, Mexico.

But this meant rowing open boats in rough Gulf waters for hundreds of miles. In their frail craft they met with one mishap after another. In the end, of the entire company that Narváez had landed in Florida, only four men survived.

Huge two-handed swords, like this one found in Texas, were used by the Spanish. On its hilt are the words: Do Not Draw Me Without Reason; Do Not Sheath Me Without Honor.

Sollerets, or steel stirrups, were part of the armor worn by Spanish cavalrymen.

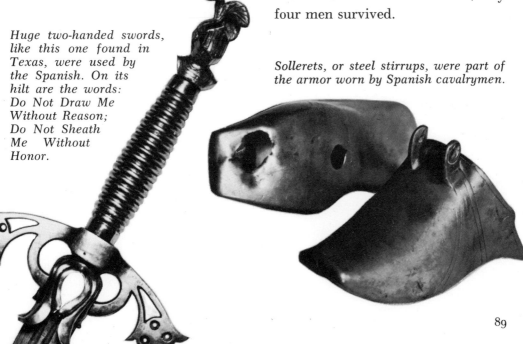

One of these was a Spanish nobleman, Alvar Núñez Cabeza de Vaca, treasurer of the expedition. What happened to him in the next eight years is one of the most amazing adventures in the whole story of America.

The five overloaded boats—between 40 and 50 men in each—coasted west as far as the mouth of the *Río del Espíritu Santo*, or the Mississippi River. There they were scattered by a storm and three ran aground with loss of all hands. The men in Cabeza de Vaca's boat rowed on, until they were cast ashore on an island near the location of Galveston, Texas. There they were joined by survivors of the fifth boat, which also had been wrecked.

The Spaniards subsisted on shellfish and the roots of water plants which were given them by friendly Indians. By the following spring, only fifteen were still alive.

The Indians believed the Spaniards were sorcerers or gods of some sort, and that if they wanted to they could cure the sick. Wrote Cabeza de Vaca:

"They wished to make us physicians without examinations or diplomas. They tried to cure themselves by breathing on each other, and with that breath and the laying of hands they hoped to make themselves well. They ordered that we also do this for them. We laughed, saying it was foolish, that we knew nothing of the art of the healer. But they insisted and withheld food from us until we did as they asked."

And so Cabeza de Vaca and his companions became medicine men to the Indians. They tried what little they knew of doctoring, and the complete faith of the natives often helped to produce good results.

The four became separated. Alone Cabeza de Vaca traveled over the vast reaches of the American southwest, shifting from one Indian tribe

Spaniards with Cabeza de Vaca probably wore equipment such as this chain-mail, sword, corselet, and morion, or helmet.

The unknown interior of America, through which Cabeza de Vaca wandered, is thronged with Indians, birds and deer on this Spanish map, made in 1551.

to another. He befriended them all. Many tribes wept when he left them.

He kept moving ever westward, hoping some day to reach the sea. West of the Sabine River, in Texas, he met again the three other survivors of Narváez's company. One was a Moorish Negro slave named Estebánico.

Together the four traveled on. They crossed Texas, where they were the first white men to marvel at the buffalo; and they were first to see the pueblos of the Hopi and Zuni Indians in New Mexico and Arizona. When they were a hundred miles from the Gulf of California they noticed that one of the Indians they met was wearing an ornament hanging from his neck. It was a buckle of a sword belt.

At the sight, Cabeza de Vaca was

so excited he could hardly speak. That buckle meant one thing—Spaniards! At last, after all the hardships he had endured, nearly seven years of seemingly endless wanderings— he had covered more than two-thirds of the distance across the United States—here was a sign of the presence of his countrymen!

The four men were told that the seashore lay to the south. They hurried on in that direction. Again they became separated, and now Cabeza de Vaca and Estebánico trudged along together. A few days later four men from the Spanish settlement of Culiacán, near the Gulf of California, suddenly halted in a road and gaped in astonishment. Before them, in company with a band of Indians, stood a Spanish-speaking white man and a Negro, looking as if they had come out of nowhere. Then Cabeza de Vaca announced who he was.

The Spaniards embraced him. Cabeza de Vaca, who had long ago given up hope of ever seeing home again, wept for joy. He was escorted to Culiacán and from there went on to Mexico City.

The travels of Cabeza de Vaca revealed to the map makers for the first time that there was an immense country lying to the north of Mexico, far broader than anyone had realized. And his stories of the "cities" or Indian pueblos which he had seen on the Plains, sent others hurrying northward from Mexico, hunting for gold.

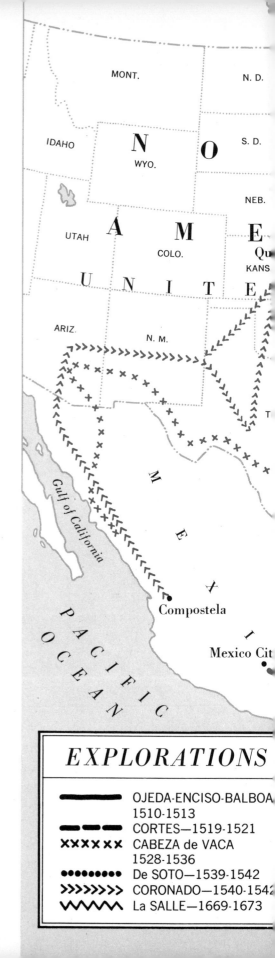

EXPLORATIONS

━━━━	OJEDA-ENCISO-BALBOA 1510-1513
━ ━ ━	CORTES—1519-1521
✕✕✕✕✕✕	CABEZA de VACA 1528-1536
●●●●●●●●	De SOTO—1539-1542
➤➤➤➤➤➤➤	CORONADO—1540-154?
〜〜〜〜〜	La SALLE—1669-1673

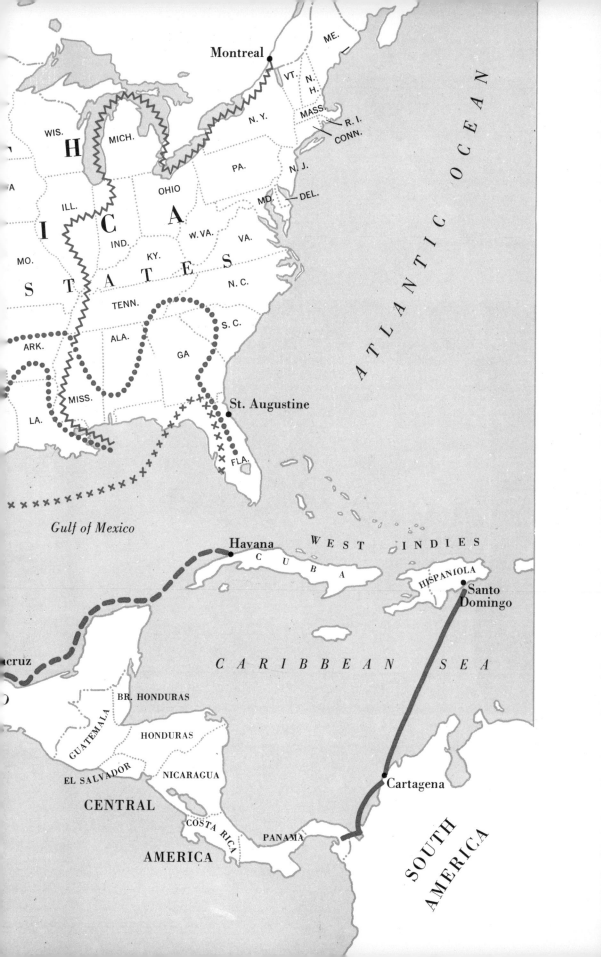

Montreal

ME.

VT. N. H.

N. Y.

MASS.

R. I.

CONN.

WIS. MICH.

PA.

N. J.

OHIO

MD. DEL.

ILL.

IND.

W. VA.

VA.

MO.

KY.

N. C.

TENN.

S. C.

ARK.

ALA.

GA.

MISS.

St. Augustine

LA.

FLA.

Gulf of Mexico

WEST INDIES

Havana

CUBA

HISPANIOLA

Santo
Domingo

cruz

CARIBBEAN SEA

BR. HONDURAS

GUATEMALA

HONDURAS

EL SALVADOR

NICARAGUA

CENTRAL

COSTA RICA

PANAMA

Cartagena

AMERICA

SOUTH
AMERICA

ATLANTIC OCEAN

Remington's painting shows Coronado's army marching across the plains of Kansas.

THE SEVEN CITIES OF GOLD

When the story of Cabeza de Vaca became known, suddenly in Mexico and Spain the numeral seven took on a magic meaning. Spaniards recalled an old legend about that number and grew as excited over it as if a great truth had just been revealed to them. This was the ancient tale:

Centuries before, the Moors of North Africa had crossed the Strait of Gibraltar and overrun Portugal and Spain. Seven Portuguese bishops, fleeing before the invaders, went to the city of Oporto and there embarked for a large island, which was supposed to move about in the Atlantic Ocean, called Antilia. On the island, which was fabulously rich, each bishop founded a city, so the legend went, and each of the seven cities had grown into a thriving metropolis.

In Mexico, an Indian slave told a story in which the seven legendary cities also figured. His father, the Indian said, had once gone on a long journey to the north, and after forty days of traveling had reached a country where there were seven great cities, all rich in gold and silver. He had come home heavily laden with treasure.

Now the Spaniards put these two stories together. The seven cities of the bishops were not on an island after all, but somewhere in the land north of Mexico. Many an adventurer in Mexico wanted to go in search of them. Before sending out a conquistador at the head of a large army, Governor Antonio de Mendoza asked a Franciscan friar, an Italian in the service of Spain, named Fray Marcos de Niza, to undertake a scouting expedition.

From Culiacán, in 1539, Fray Marcos went north to the valley of the Sonora River in the northwest corner of Mexico, then through what is now Arizona. Along the way he learned from the Indians that there were indeed seven cities. They were in a country farther on, called Cibola. The houses were of stone, he was told, some of them four and five stories high, and the doorways and

window frames were richly ornamented with turquoise. Cibola, he was told, was a thirty-day march to the north. The way led into western New Mexico.

When he was a few miles from Cibola the friar climbed a hill and gazed across the country. In the blue distance, shining in the sun, was the hazy skyline of what looked like a noble city. At last—Cibola! Number one of the seven! And how grand it looked, even from this far away! "The city from where I beheld it looked splendid," Fray Marcos wrote. "It is certainly the handsomest one I have seen in all these parts. The houses are of stone. As well as I could judge, it is even larger than the city of Mexico."

But he had not judged very well. The distance and his own eager imagination had played tricks on him. Actually what he had seen was a large pueblo of the Zunis—a terraced village with walls of adobe, or sun-

This detail, from a 1590 De Bry map, attempts to picture the Plains Indians and buffalo as described by Coronado's men.

95

Ácoma, "The City of the Sky", is one of the Indian villages Coronado visited in 1540. Its sandstone cliffs kept it safe until 1599, when it fell to the Spanish.

hardened mud held together by a cement made from ashes. There were within it two hundred primitive dwellings, housing altogether about one thousand persons.

Fray Marcos' report swept through Mexico like a whirlwind. Again the Spaniards began dreaming of gold and glory. Even the wise and careful Governor Mendoza believed he might have within his reach another Mexico, another Peru, maybe even more! He decided to send an expedition as quickly as possible. To lead it he chose one of the top men in his government, a nobleman named Francisco Vásquez de Coronado.

It was a colorful procession, heavily armed, lavishly equipped, that Coronado led out of Mexico City in the year 1540. There were 225 mounted Spaniards, mostly young gentlemen carrying long lances, and decked out in silks and velvets of bright blue, red, and gold. Their polished armor flashed in the sun. Plumes bobbed on the helmets of the caballeros. They were accompanied by 1,000 Indians, who drove before them great herds of cattle and pigs to be used for food.

They made their way to a Spanish settlement called Culiacán. But long before they had completed this

This photograph pictures the deserted New Mexican pueblo as it appears today.

horsemen and a few foot soldiers. Continuing northward, they crossed what is now the border of the United States into the desert lands of Arizona, then on to an Indian village near the present town of Gallup, New Mexico. Now they were a few days' march from the first "great city" of the fabled province of Cibola —actually, the Zuni pueblo that Fray Marcos had viewed from a distant hilltop.

The little army paused for a few days to rest, taking the food that was stored in the village. The Indians knew all too well the dread power of guns and crossbows.

Nevertheless, the village chieftain stood up bravely, desperately, to a group of the white invaders. With a stick he drew a line on the ground.

first leg of the journey the young gentlemen began to grumble about the hardships of travel in that country. As the weeks passed, their fine clothes became stained and dusty. The heavy armor was tiring as the warm weather set in.

Two months after leaving Mexico City they reached Culiacán. Here Coronado decided to take only part of his army ahead, leaving the main force with instructions to follow in a few weeks. He set out with fifty

This modern portrait of Coronado was based on descriptions of the conquistador. No contemporary picture exists.

Martines' map of 1578 pictures the seven imaginary Cities of Cibola close to the

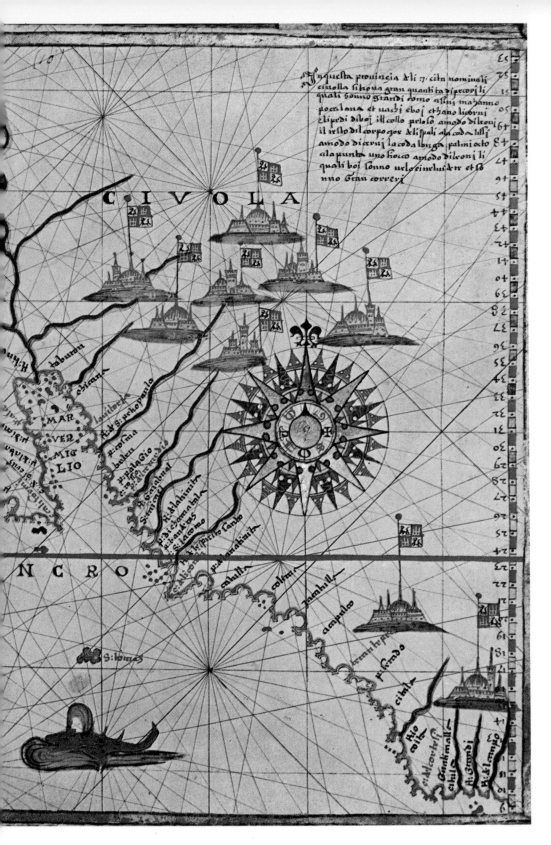

Gulf of California (labeled "The Vermilion Sea"). Nearby are China and Japan.

Beyond this, he warned, they must not step. Contemptuously, one of the Spaniards spurred his horse toward the line. The horse, as if possessed of better sense than its rider, reared back, but an arrow felled it. Another brought down the soldier. Then the other Spaniards charged.

It was all over a few minutes later. Not only did the white men win the skirmish; as punishment they hanged every man, woman, and child in the village.

The Indians farther along fought back, even when they knew they had no chance of winning. They captured rattlesnakes and put them in wooden cages. They poked arrows into the cages and teased the snakes until they would bite at the arrowheads and cover them with poison. They let the poison dry, then shot the arrows at the Spaniards.

At last Coronado and his men came to the place that Fray Marcos had described as the "great city" of Cibola. And what a crushing disappointment it was! Instead of handsome buildings and wealth and grandeur rivaling Mexico itself they saw only a mud-walled pueblo!

Coronado was bitter and angry, and the young men of his army were so furious with Fray Marcos that the friar decided it was not safe to remain with them and quietly disappeared to return to Mexico.

Coronado remained at the pueblo, waiting for the main part of his army to come from Culiacán. In the meantime he sent out men in small groups to explore the country.

What Coronado's scouts learned about this country was not encouraging. One after another, they came back with the same story— more pueblos, some decorated pottery, patterned cloth, but nothing to make this long journey worthwhile to a Spaniard—no cities, no gold or jewels or silver.

But Coronado would not give up. When the main body of the army arrived at the pueblo, he told his lieutenants to hold it there while he set forth with another party of explorers. He turned to the east and south and traveled many days into what is now the plains of Texas.

Doggedly, day after day, Coronado went on with the search. But the land was as bare as it was big, and the farther he went the more hopeless the task became. The men lost heart. Coronado himself, stubborn as he was, might have turned back, had it not been for an Indian who had come along with the army from Cibola and who told new and marvelous tales of great riches ahead.

The Spaniards nicknamed this Indian "the Turk" because he wore a headdress which looked like a turban. The seven cities were in his native country, he said, a country called Quivira. It was far, far away, a march of many weeks. The ruler of Quivira took his afternoon nap under a tree hung with hundreds of little gold bells that lulled him to sleep

The Quivira which Coronado found in Kansas was only a group of thatched huts. It probably looked much like this Wichita Indian village, sketched in 1852.

as they tinkled in the breeze. And even the common people of Quivira had quantities of gold, said the Turk —so much that they ate from golden bowls and drank from golden jugs.

As Coronado listened to these marvelous tales, his hopes revived. He would let the Turk lead him to Quivira. For many weeks during the year 1541 the Turk led them on, over the wide, grassy prairies, across countless streams, and from one Indian village to another, north and east toward the middle of the land that is now the United States.

But nowhere did they see their dream come true, nor even any promising signs. Finally they called a halt and asked the natives where Quivira was. They were told it was a march of 40 days to the north. Coronado picked 30 of his best men to go on with him to Quivira. With his little group he resumed the journey. By this time he suspected that the Turk had been lying. Again he took the

Turk with him, but this time in chains.

At last, after crossing Oklahoma into Kansas and continuing eastward, the Spaniards arrived at the place which the Indians called Quivira. Today nobody knows its exact location. But one thing is certain: Quivira was nothing but a spot on the immense plains where the wolves howled around a thin scattering of rude huts with roofs of straw.

Halting in that wild, windswept curve of bare horizons in the middle

Walpi pueblo, in Arizona, glows like a city of gold in the brilliance of the setting sun. Sights like this probably helped mislead Fray Marcos and Coronado into believing fabulous accounts of the golden cities of Cibola and Quivira.

of America, many hundreds of miles from home, Coronado and his men knew at last what they should have known many months before—that they had been tricked.

One last time, Coronado questioned the Turk. And now the Turk admitted he had been lying from the beginning. His people, the red men, wanted to destroy these white invaders who had robbed them of their food and killed so many of them. The Turk explained that he and his brother tribesmen could not hope to drive the white men out of their country by fighting them. Therefore he had conceived the idea of playing on their greed for gold and of leading them on such a long, hard trip that the horses would be weakened and the men left to starve on the empty plains.

Immediately, on orders from Coronado, two Spaniards dragged the Turk away, wrapped a rope around his neck, and choked him to death.

But there was little satisfaction in that for the infuriated Spaniards. In 1542, Coronado went home to Mexico a broken man, empty-handed after more than two years of searching in America for gold. About a hundred of his men went home with him. The others deserted, scattered, and returned their separate ways. And thus ended one of the longest marches in history, from Mexico City more than 3,000 miles into the very heartland of America.

A PASSAGE
TO THE INDIES

When Cabeza de Vaca went home to Spain he received an invitation to visit Hernando de Soto, who had served under Pizarro in Peru. The returns from that adventure, added to de Soto's own fortune, had made him one of the richest men in all Spain—so rich indeed that the King himself had begun borrowing money from him.

De Soto had a special reason for wanting to talk with Cabeza de Vaca. Just three months before, he had obtained from the King the right to explore the huge expanse of the North American mainland which at that time was called Florida—the whole southeastern part of what is now the United States—and to set up a colony there and rule over it.

De Soto questioned Cabeza de Vaca closely about Florida. He explained that he was planning a great expedition, and invited Cabeza de Vaca to go with him. Cabeza de Vaca politely declined.

Now de Soto felt sure his uncommunicative guest must have plans of his own with respect to Florida. Very likely, the story of the seven cities was true. In the ancient legend, the seven cities were somewhere on

This portrait of Hernando de Soto was based on a picture made during his lifetime. The original painting is now lost.

the coast of an island sea, or on a strait, or on the banks of a great river linking the Gulf of Mexico with the Pacific Ocean. Somewhere in Florida, de Soto believed he would find that waterway, and so discover another land as wealthy as the lands of the Aztecs and Incas.

He was so sure of this that he was willing to gamble his own money on it. The King of Spain was quite willing to let him do so. De Soto spent a year getting his ships ready.

It was a very elaborate expedition that he brought together. In it were 600 men, most of them high-ranking nobles of Castile. Among them was a scattering of seasoned army veterans. It was also a very costly enterprise. Nine ships were needed, along with an impressive array of arms, hundreds of horses, packs of hounds to be loosed upon defiant Indians, herds of cattle and pigs, and immense stocks of food and supplies. By the time all this was provided, Hernando de Soto had put his whole fortune into the expedition.

Some of the officers took along their wives and children and left them in Havana, Cuba, the first port of call. Late in May, 1539, the army was set ashore on the east coast of the Florida peninsula.

De Soto began his search at once. For the next six months he combed through the country in the western part of what is now the state of Florida, looking for signs of gold mines, for cities, and for waterways.

He found nothing. As in the past, the Indians of Florida fought desperately to drive the white invaders away. But de Soto was tougher than those who had come before him. He ruthlessly attacked the natives. A Spanish chronicler of the time, named Oviedo, who knew de Soto well, said he "was very fond of the sport of killing Indians." He did not hesitate to risk his own life or the lives of his men. As they fought their way through one Indian town after

another—burning many to the ground and leaving corpses for the wolves—they suffered serious losses themselves. In two of these skirmishes de Soto was badly wounded. But everywhere, the final outcome was the same—the guns and cross-bows, the steel blades, the blood-hounds, the charging horses, proved too much for the Indians.

For four years the company of hungry, ragged noblemen went doggedly on, searching the forests, swamps, canebrakes, hills, and river bottoms, the endless wilderness of "Florida," looking in vain for the golden harvest of their dreams. They covered a wide expanse of unexplored North America—from Florida to Georgia, South Carolina and North Carolina; across the Appalachians into Tennessee, Alabama and Mississippi; and westward across the Mississippi River into Arkansas, Oklahoma and Texas. How far north de Soto went up the Mississippi is not known exactly, but he probably was within 200 miles of the Missouri.

In the summer of 1541 the remnant of his expedition was only a few days away, by Indian runner, from the army of Coronado. Coronado heard of his party and sent a message, but the courier failed to locate de Soto's army.

Wherever they went, de Soto and his men left behind them a trail of misery, starvation, and death. At a town near modern Mobile, Alabama, an Indian chief tried to turn the

De Soto was not the first to penetrate the eastern wilderness north of Florida, for in 1526, Lucas Vasquez de Ayllón had attempted a colony in North Carolina, which had to be abandoned. But even after Coronado and de Soto's travels, in the 1540's, the rest of Europe knew practically nothing about the interior of North America. The detail from a French map made in 1550 (above) by Desceliers, is sprinkled with legendary unicorns and pygmies hunting flamingoes. Some of the earliest pictures to give a realistic view of the Indians de Soto saw, in Mississippi and Louisiana, were made in 1735, by a Frenchman named DeBatz. His water-color (below) shows an Atakapa Indian (right) with his women and slaves.

DeBatz' watercolor pictures Choctaw Indians of Alabama and Mississippi. Similarly painted warriors, carrying scalps on poles, may have been seen by de Soto.

tables on de Soto. He invited the Spaniard to sit down with him in one of the houses of the walled town and have a friendly talk. The main part of the Spanish army remained outside the gates. Meanwhile Indian warriors, with bows and arrows ready, were hiding in ambush inside.

Against the advice of his officers, de Soto took a few men with him and went in. At a signal from the chief, the warriors sprang out and attacked the little group of Spaniards. De Soto ran for his life before a shower of arrows. Twice he fell, the second time with an ugly wound, but he managed to reach the army outside. Five companions died.

De Soto ordered the town surrounded and set afire. The Indians were trapped inside. Spanish soldiers stationed at the gates barred their escape while others dashed in to finish them off. The red men fought to the last. By nightfall 2,000 were dead, killed by the weapons of the Spaniards or by rushing into the flaming houses when they could fight no longer. Twenty Spaniards lost their lives and 150 were wounded.

After a long rest to recover from their injuries the Spaniards resumed their march, swinging northwest, and hacking and slogging their way through hundreds of miles of thick woods and swamp lands of Alabama and Mississippi. The winter was bitter cold and the Indians were constantly harassing the Spaniards. But de Soto was too proud to return to the coast and wait for his ships to rescue him.

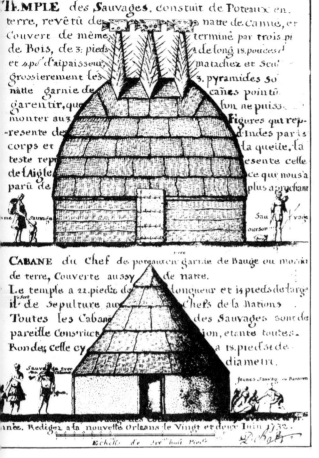

In 1732, DeBatz pictured a temple and cabin of the Acolapissa Indians of the lower Mississippi valley. Structures were made of wooden posts covered with cane matting. The walls of the chief's cabin (below) were coated with clay. Similar houses were built by the Cherokees and Choctaws visited by de Soto.

In May, 1541, in northern Mississippi, about thirty miles south of the site of Memphis, Tennessee, he reached the "great river." One of his men later wrote that it was so wide that "a man standing on the opposite shore could not have been recognized as a man." Watching the trees and heavy tangles of driftwood that were carried down on its mighty current,

de Soto's company knew this was no ordinary stream.

What they were out to discover was not great rivers but gold and a strait to the Pacific. The Mississippi was just a big water barrier blocking their path. So they spent a month building four barges, crossed the river, and took up their search on the other side without paying any further respects whatever to the mighty "Father of Waters."

After more months of fruitless wanderings that took them as far west as Texas, the company dug in for the winter in the valley of the Arkansas River. By spring of the year 1542 they were deep in despair. Three years they had spent searching, but they had found nothing. They had lost 250 men. Their gunpowder was gone, their supplies low, their clothes in tatters. Again the winter had proved rugged. The dwindling army had suffered severely from cold and hunger.

De Soto decided at last to go to the sea and try to reach Mexico. Through March and April he made his way down the valley of the Arkansas. But instead of bringing him out on the shore of the Gulf of Mexico, as he had hoped, this course took him back to the Mississippi River, hundreds of miles north of the Gulf.

At the site of modern Natchez, Mississippi, he came down with a fever. Spent in body and spirit, he took to his pallet, lay there a month, and died. His men, afraid that if the Indians were to find out he was dead they would feel encouraged to attack again, hid the body.

The Indians noticed, however, that the white men's leader was missing. When they asked about him, they were told that de Soto had gone up into the sky—a thing he was in the habit of doing from time to time —and that he would be back soon.

Secretly, in the dark of night, the Spaniards wrapped the body in blankets woven of buffalo hair, weighted it with sand, and took it out onto the river. There the little company of armed cavaliers and hooded priests, standing in a torch-lit canoe, committed the body to the depths of the great river.

What was left of the army decided to try for Mexico by marching west-

ward. All summer the survivors plodded on, but after covering hundreds of miles they gave up hope and went back to the Mississippi. They built boats, stole a few canoes, and started down the 700 miles of river to the Gulf.

It was a hazardous dash for escape, the last hope of desperate men. Some drowned when the canoes overturned. Others were felled as their boats ran the gauntlet of arrows shot from the riverbanks.

Next came the grueling task of rowing for hundreds of miles from the mouth of the Mississippi along the coast of the Gulf of Mexico. At last, many months later, they made in at the Spanish settlement of Pánuco, Mexico. Of the 600 men who had landed with Hernando de Soto

De Soto's route through the southeast was traced on Delisle's map of 1737.

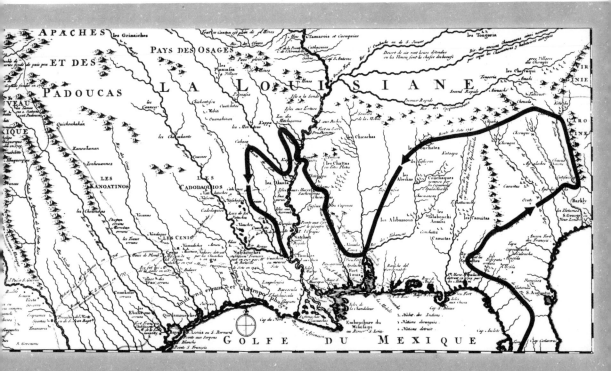

in Florida, only 311 were still alive.

Of their arrival at Pánuco, one of them wrote: "Many, leaping ashore, kissed the ground; and all, on bended knees, with hands raised above them and eyes turned toward heaven, again and again gave thanks to God."

Thus ended the great gamble that Hernando de Soto had felt so sure he could win. To undertake it he had

Remington's painting shows de Soto's army floundering through the swamps as it approaches the Mississippi River.

With the tragic failures of Coronado and de Soto, Spain gave up forever the quest of the seven mythical cities of Cibola, and for the next forty years Spanish adventurers contented themselves mainly with shipping home the wealth they extracted from the West Indies, Mexico, and South America.

While Coronado and de Soto were penetrating overland to the heart of the continent, Governor Mendoza of Mexico continued to probe for the elusive strait which would unite the Atlantic and the Pacific. He wanted to see if it could be located at its western end by exploring the American west coast. He placed two ships in command of Juan Rodríguez Cabrillo, a Portuguese navigator in the service of Spain, and sent him sailing northward.

In 1542, Cabrillo sailed along the California coast as far as San Francisco Bay, took sick there, and died. His pilot, Bartolomé Ferrelo, carried on in command of the little fleet, continued north to the coast of southern Oregon, and then turned back because the ships were no longer seaworthy. With Cabrillo and his pilot reporting no sign of a water route across America to the Indies, Spanish explorers were forced to give up that hope, too.

sold his palace in Seville and invested one of the largest fortunes in Spain. At his death his entire estate consisted of five Indian slaves, three horses, and a herd of pigs.

THE DIAMONDS
OF CANADA

Jacques Cartier was an able sailor from the port of St. Malo in Brittany, France, whence scores of fishing vessels were regularly crossing the Atlantic each year to the Grand Banks off Newfoundland. Backed by King Francis I, Cartier sailed on April 20, 1534, with 61 men, in two tiny caravels, which carried four cannon apiece. One of his chief purposes was to look for the route to India through the northern part of America.

Cartier reached the east coast of Newfoundland, stopped to repair his ships, then sailed through the Strait of Belle Isle into the Gulf of St. Lawrence. With high hopes of finding his way westward through the continent, he crossed the Gulf. He was "grieved and heartsick" to find his way blocked by the western end of Chaleur Bay.

He befriended two men, sons of an Iroquois chief who lived where Montreal is now. They served as guides. These Indians spoke of "Canada," their homeland, and of a glorious country, far to the west, which they called Saguenay. From their description of Saguenay, "where people were rich and wore clothes like his

On the "Island of Birds" in the Gulf of St. Lawrence, Cartier's men might have seen Indians killing puffins and auks.

own," Cartier wondered whether he was hearing about some part of the realm of the Great Khan of Cathay.

In his search of the Gulf of St. Lawrence, Cartier entered the channel between the island of Anticosti and the shore of Labrador.

Here the current ran so swift against him at ebb tide that the ships were driven back. Even when he put over the long-boat, with thirteen men pulling at the oars, "it was impossible to make headway."

At this difficult point the summer was nearly over and supplies were running low. Cartier decided to go home. He took the two Indians with him to France.

In May of the following year he set sail again for America. Francis I gave him three ships—the *Grande Hermine* of 120 tons, the *Petite Hermine* of 60 tons, and a 40-ton pinnace. This time Cartier made the whole circuit of the gulf, and again was disappointed. Nowhere was there anything that even looked like a strait until he came back to the mouth of the St. Lawrence River.

The Indians told him, however, that this was not a way to another sea; that it was a river; that the 75-mile wide estuary became narrow farther on; and that the water turned fresh. They said the river would lead to their home, which they called Hochelaga, and that to the north lay the wonderful country of Saguenay. Cartier decided to sail up the river.

Everywhere, the Indians were friendly—sometimes begging the Frenchmen to remain with them. Before the travelers they heaped huge offerings of deer meat, fresh fish, maize, fruits, nuts, hides, whale oil, and ivory of walrus tusks.

At a town near where Quebec is now, the chief, whose name was Donnacona, tried to persuade Cartier not to go on to Hochelaga. He offered slaves as a bribe, and when that failed, tried a curious trick.

Cartier's flagship, the Grande Hermine, *from a sketch in a Canadian history of 1701. The large number of cannon shown here are an exaggeration.*

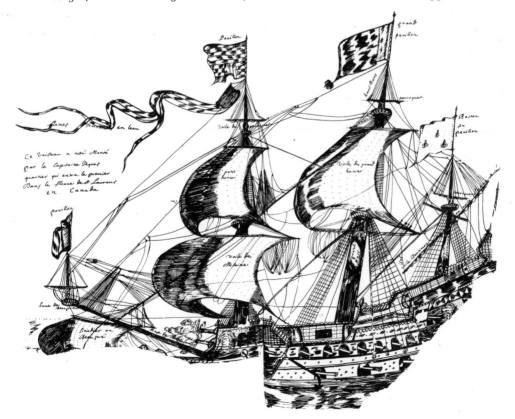

113

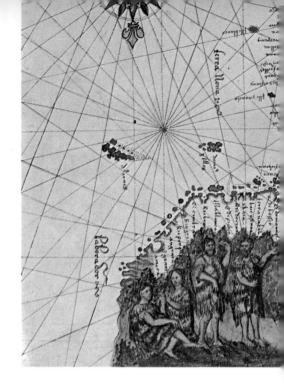

Cartier, wearing a red doublet and a black cloak, is surrounded by his party at the mouth of the St. Lawrence River, in this detail on a French map of 1542. Lurking in the forests are bears, and fur-clad Indians hunting elk and deer.

Suddenly one night three Indians appeared before Cartier. They were dressed in black and white dog skins, their faces were blackened, and they carried long horns on their heads. Gravely they explained that they were devils, sent by a god to warn Cartier not to go to Hochelaga. If he did, they said, the god would make ice and snow there and all the Frenchmen would freeze to death! Cartier answered that he trusted in his own God to keep him safe. He took his leave and a few weeks later arrived at Hochelaga, a walled town of the Iroquois, made up of fifty large houses.

The natives hailed the white men as gods and brought their sick and their crippled before Cartier, asking him to lay hands on them and make them well. Cartier read to them from the Bible, prayed for them, and passed out gifts among them.

Near the village was a great hill which he climbed and named Mont Réal (Mount Royal). From the top he could view the land for many miles around. "It was flat and arable, the finest country one could expect to see anywhere in the world," he

This 16th century portrait of Jacques Cartier is preserved in Paris, France.

114

wrote. "As far as the eye could reach, I beheld the broad river flowing through it. . . . There were four stretches of rapids, but beyond these one could navigate at least three moons farther."

But again the cold weather was coming on. Cartier went down-river, back to Quebec, and the company settled for the winter.

In the long, cold months, with no more fresh vegetables or fruits, the men came down with scurvy. But from the Indians Cartier learned how to fight off that disease by drinking an infusion made from the needles of evergreen trees.

Chief Donnacona spent many a winter evening telling Cartier about the glories of Saguenay. To explore Saguenay properly, Cartier decided, he would need a whole new expedition. In order to obtain help from

King Francis, Cartier decided to take Donnacona to France and let him tell the king about the wonders Saguenay held. As the time drew near for his return voyage, Cartier kidnaped Donnacona and a few of his friends, but promised to bring them safely home in a few months.

In Paris he found King Francis hard pressed for money and reluctant to risk a large sum on another expedition to America. Cartier encouraged Chief Donnacona to describe Saguenay to the King.

Donnacona did his best. He told King Francis that he had visited the land of Saguenay and with his own eyes had seen there "immense quantities of gold, rubies, and other rich things."

The King was deeply impressed. However, it was not until several years later that he provided money

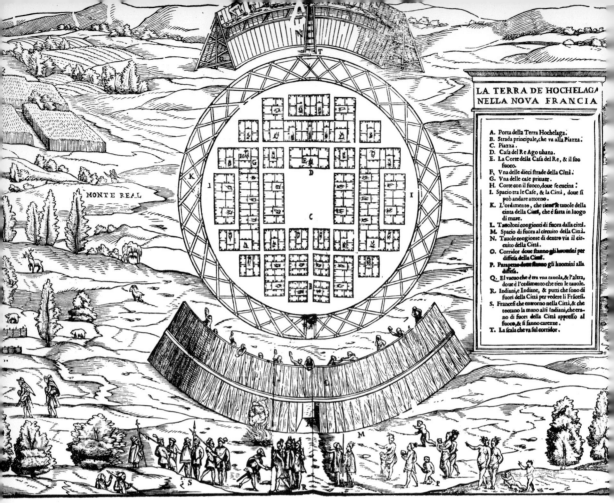

Within the image, the following labels appear:

MONTE REAL

LA TERRA DE HOCHELAGA
NELLA NOVA FRANCIA

A. Porta della Terra Hochelaga.
B. Strada principale, che va alla Piazza.
C. Piazza.
D. Casa del Re Ago uhana.
E. La Corte della Casa del Re, & il suo
   fuoco.
F. Vna delle dieci strade della Città.
G. Vna delle case priuate.
H. Corte con il fuoco, doue se cucina.
I. Spacio tra le Case, & la Città, doue si
   può andare attorno.
K. L'ordimento, che tiene le tauole della
   cinta della Città, che è fatta in luogo
   di mure.
L. Tauoloni congionti di fuora dalla città.
M. Spacio di fuora al circuito della Città.
N. Tauole congionte di dentro via il cir-
   cuito della Città.
O. Corridor doue stanno gli huomini per
   difesa della Città.
P. Parapetto doue stanno gli huomini alla
   difesa.
Q. El vacuo che è tra vna tauola, & l'altra,
   doue è l'ordimento che tien le tauole.
R. Indiani, Indiane, & putti che sono di
   fuori della Città per vedere li Francesi.
S. Francesi che entorno nella Città, & che
   toccano la mano alli Indiani, che era-
   no di fuori della Città appresso al
   fuoco, & si fanno carezze.
T. La scala che va sul corridor.

Hochelaga, the walled village of the Iroquois Indians, was visited by Cartier in 1535. It stood on the St. Lawrence River, where Montreal is now located.

to send Cartier to America again. Meantime, Donnacona died in France.

It was an elaborate enterprise that Cartier led on his third voyage to Canada, for the purpose of establishing the colony of New France in America. The King gave him ten ships and assigned more than a thousand people to the joint expedition which he and Jean François de la Rocque, Sieur de Roberval, were to head. As Roberval was delayed, Cartier sailed alone, with five ships, in May, 1541.

When Cartier returned to the site of Hochelaga, the village he had known before had disappeared, and he found only a deserted clearing in the woods. Nearby stood a new Indian village made up of people he had never seen before.

He did not even try to reach Saguenay. Instead, he returned to Quebec, spent the winter near that town, and in the summer of 1542 sailed back to France because he found the Indians hostile—and perhaps also because of an exciting discovery he made at a spot close to the site of his winter headquarters.

What he had found was a mine. And there he dug up what he believed to be a great treasure—several barrels of "gold ore" and "silver ore" and bushel-basketsful of "precious stones, rubies, and diamonds."

Actually what the mine yielded was "fool's gold"—iron pyrites that showed as yellowish metal in the rock—mica which looked like diamonds, and crystals of corundum, or aluminum oxide, resembling rubies and sapphires.

It was only after he had returned to France that he learned he had brought home a load of rubbish. Ever since that day the French people have had a saying, a phrase they use to suggest fake or fraud—"*Voilà un diamant de Canada!*—That's a Canadian diamond!"

And so, in the year 1543, the same that brought to an end the search by the Spaniards for a sea-strait through the continent of North America, the French gave up their quest for the same strait in Canada, and did no more organized exploration for nearly sixty years.

Gastaldi's map of New France, showing part of the Gulf of St. Lawrence, was published in 1556. This area, including Newfoundland and Nova Scotia was visited in 1603 by Champlain's patron, Pierre du Guast, Count de Monts.

CHAMPLAIN'S NEW FRANCE

In the sixteenth century, the future of America was considerably influenced by the style of a hat.

When fishermen working on the Grand Banks of Newfoundland sailed into the Gulf of St. Lawrence, one of the few items of value which the natives could offer in exchange for the white men's knives and axes was the fur of the beaver. Felt could be made of the fine hair of the beaver, and a hat made of this felt not only was very handsome but would last for many years.

Rich Europeans prized their beaver hats. Men began going to America to trade with the Indians for beaver skins. Long after Spanish and French explorers had given up their search for a strait to the Pacific Ocean, the Canadian fur trade kept on growing.

By 1600, it had become so profitable that big businessmen of France were vying with each other for a monopoly on this trade. But the French king, Henry IV, wanted to claim land in America, and to send Frenchmen there to live on it. The King therefore decreed that if any company of businessmen wanted the

monopoly on the fur trade, it would have to found a colony in America.

A company was formed for this purpose. The first thing it did was to send an expert in geography to look over the country where the furs came from. The man chosen for this was 31-year-old Samuel de Champlain— a man who was to become one of the most important figures in the early exploration of North America.

When Champlain made his first voyage to the St. Lawrence in 1603

north say that from their homes they can look at a sea which is salt. I hold that if this be so, it is some gulf of this our sea [the Atlantic] which overflows into the north in the middle of the continent."

His guess was correct. The "gulf of this our sea" was Hudson Bay, which Henry Hudson was to discover seven years later.

Champlain spent three months going over the same general area that Cartier had covered. Just above Montreal he was stopped by the Lachine Rapids in the St. Lawrence River.

Having no canoe, he had to turn back. At Tadoussac he traded with the Indians, loaded his ship with a valuable cargo of furs, and departed for France.

On Champlain's return, his reports of the wonderful country across the Atlantic stirred up such excitement that two more ships were sent out to America. Champlain went again— this time as the King's geographer.

For the next five years he explored the St. Lawrence country, Nova Scotia, and the land to the southwest that was soon to be known as New England. From Cape Breton Island to southern Massachusetts he charted the coast line and made friends with the Indians.

The search for a place to build a settlement took him back to the St.

there was no European settlement anywhere along the eastern seaboard of North America north of the Spanish outposts in Florida.

On reaching the St. Lawrence, Champlain stopped at a town of the Indians called Tadoussac, then continued upstream to the Saguenay River.

After talking with some Indians who arrived there with furs to trade, Champlain wrote:

"These said savages from the

Samuel de Champlain.

Lawrence in his ship *Le Don de Dieu* —or the *Gift of God*. To a place on the great river which the Indians called Rebec (or "a narrowing of the waters")—came many canoes laden with beaver, marten and other skins to be bartered to the white men. Here, in 1608, on a jutting headland, Champlain laid the foundations for Quebec, the first important French settlement.

For generations, the Algonquins of the country to the north of the river had been under attack by the warlike Iroquois from the south.

Champlain, by nature a man of peace, found himself forced to take sides. He chose to ally himself with the people who were his neighbors and who did business with him, the Algonquins and other nations of the northern group.

Champlain had heard about a big lake to the south, which was said to be dotted with beautiful islands and to lie in the midst of a rich, fertile country. From the St. Lawrence it could be reached by canoeing up the Richelieu River. He had long wanted to make a visit of peaceful exploration to that area. But in 1609 the Huron Indians demanded that he go along with their war party and help them conquer the Iroquois.

Only three Frenchmen—Champlain himself and two soldiers—accompanied the 60 warriors in their canoes as they paddled southward to the lake. The three white men carried harquebuses—forerunners of the shotgun.

After cruising on the lake for three weeks they came upon a large fleet of Iroquois canoes.

The next morning the two parties clashed on the shore of the lake. As the arrows began to fly, Champlain, in the vanguard of the northern force, fired a shot from his harquebus. The two soldiers, from a position at the side, did the same. Three enemy warriors fell dead.

The Mohawks were terrified by the roar of the guns and the sight of their fallen tribesmen. To a man, they made for the woods, and the Indians from Quebec performed a dance of victory on the spot.

The results of this expedition were important to the white men as well as to the Indians. Champlain had surveyed the whole length of the

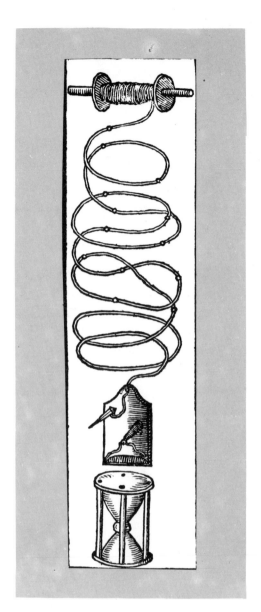

lake. As its discoverer, he claimed for France the entire area for 150 miles in all directions. The beautiful body of water still bears the name, Lake Champlain.

A few years later Champlain's Indian friends, the Algonquins, came to him with another war plan. They would strike a great blow at the Iroquois, by attacking a strong fortress of the enemy a thousand miles away near the present town of Oneida in central New York State. They needed Champlain to act as their leader.

Champlain knew that this adventure would give him a chance to explore unknown regions to the west and south where he had heard there were great fresh-water seas. He decided to go.

In July, 1615, he set out with a small group of the war party—a French servant, an interpreter, and ten Indians, traveling in two canoes. They paddled up the Ottawa River, then west into Georgian Bay on Lake Huron.

The route the Indians had chosen now swung back sharply to the eastern end of Lake Ontario, and then inland through New York State to a point near Lake Oneida. Here, three months after leaving Quebec, Champlain waited while other groups of

his Indian allies arrived on the scene. Then, with a greatly enlarged fighting force, he advanced on the big fortress of the Iroquois.

The moment his Indians came in sight of it, however, they attacked recklessly and without plan.

Although many Iroquois inside the fort were killed or wounded by the guns of the French, the losses

BAYE
D'HVTSON

CARTE
pour servir a l'eclaircissement
du Papier Terrier
DE LA NOUVELLE FRANCE

LAC

HU-

LAC ONTARIO

RON   LAC
HERIE

*The wildlife that made Canada so valu-
able, and the Indians who roamed its
trackless wilderness are pictured on this
map of New France. It was made in 1678,
43 years after Champlain's death; and it
is dedicated to Jean Baptiste Colbert,
the chief minister to King Louis XIV.*

suffered by the attacking Algonquins and Hurons were much larger.
After several days of battle Champlain's forces retreated.

Champlain himself was wounded.
His Indians carried him off in a bas-

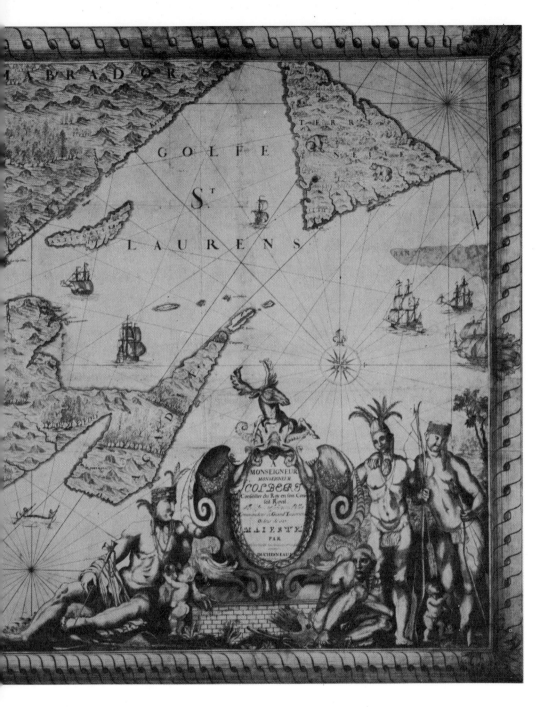

ket. He stayed through the winter in the care of the Hurons on the shore of Lake Ontario. When the trails were passable in the spring, he returned to Quebec.

Business at the trading post kept him from further adventures of discovery. He sent out young assistants, always with the reminder to look for the strait or the inland sea which he had never given up hope of finding. These young men explored the

Champlain's home in Quebec was this fortified dwelling, called the "Abitation." Here he died on Christmas Day, 1635, in the city he had founded 27 years before.

land in many directions and added much to Europe's knowledge of what is now the United States, as far west as the Great Lakes and the Mississippi River and from Canada south to the Chesapeake Bay.

The French, including Champlain himself, were not satisfied with Quebec as a colony. In 1620, it was still nothing more than a trading post, with only 50 Frenchmen living there. Meanwhile the English had planted colonies in Jamestown, Virginia, and Plymouth, Massachusetts; and by 1625, the Dutch had established a trading post in New Amsterdam.

Paris, which had never been willing to give Champlain as much support as he needed, finally realized that New France might lose out in the race with rival powers.

Shortly thereafter England went to war with France, and British warships invaded the St. Lawrence.

On July 19, 1629, Champlain was forced to surrender Quebec. He and his colonists were taken to England as prisoners of war. But on arriving home, their captors learned the war was already over, and Champlain returned to France.

This interruption almost ended the life of New France. Champlain spent much of his time in Paris trying to get more backing for his colony. He wanted settlers and a large armed force to help him bring about the defeat of the Iroquois.

He failed to get the assistance he asked of his own government. But he went back to Canada in 1632, resolved to build up the colony again. He found that the Indians welcomed him with great joy.

Champlain could explore no more, but he kept sending out his young men. One of them, Jean Nicolet, reached Lake Michigan and followed the shore to Green Bay, north of what is now Chicago. Before he left Quebec, Nicolet packed among his equipment an embroidered robe "of China damask, all strewn with flowers and birds of many colors"—just in case he should find, as he continued west, that he was within the borders of Cathay!

Other young men and Christian missionaries worked in the cause of New France in many distant places, but Champlain did not live to witness their achievements. He died in 1635, two years after his return to Quebec, mourned by red man and white man alike.

Champlain fires his harquebus at the Iroquois, supported by his Algonquin and Huron Indian allies. This "Battle of Ticonderoga," fought in the summer of 1609 on the shore of Lake Champlain, made the Iroquois permanent enemies of France.

John White's watercolor, made in the 1580's, shows Eskimos in kayaks attacking English sailors. Hudson and Frobisher must have seen similar sights.

A NORTHWEST PASSAGE

By the early 1600's, every important dent in America's east coast, every likely-looking bay and inlet and river, had been explored by men who were looking for the beginning of a way through to China, except in one part—the far north.

After Cabot's discovery of the continent, it had taken the British nearly eighty years to become interested in America again. In 1576, more than thirty years after Cartier had given up, England began looking for the northwest passage in earnest.

An English soldier set aside his sword and took to reading books on geography. He was Sir Humphrey Gilbert, a half-brother of Sir Walter Raleigh. The more he read about America and the longer he pored over maps of the New World, the more firmly was Sir Humphrey convinced that America was an island and that along the northern shore of that island lay the way for ships to sail west to the Orient.

"This discovery," he wrote, "hath been reserved for some noble prince or worthie man, to make himselfe rich, and the new world happie."

He got permission from Queen Elizabeth to send a daring sea captain, Martin Frobisher, to the far north. The Queen and her friends invested money in the venture.

Three times, in as many years beginning in 1576, Frobisher crossed the Atlantic and braved the Arctic wastes. He explored a deep indentation which is still called Frobisher Bay. Here, as he sailed westward into the long, narrow indentation for more than 150 miles with land on both sides, he believed that the shore to his left was America and that the one to his right was Asia. He did not continue far enough to discover that this "channel" tapered to a closed end, and so returned to England believing he had found the passage to the Indies.

One of his men, going ashore, brought back a piece of black stone. On their return to England, an "expert" in London examined it and pronounced it gold.

Frobisher was sent across again with instructions to bring back more of the black ore. He returned with nearly 200 tons of it—whereupon

the metal was found to be "fool's gold" of no value! All the people who had invested lost their money, but not before Frobisher was sent out again on a third voyage.

This time he entered what later became known as Hudson Strait, which would have led him into Hudson Bay. But here, thinking he had made a mistake, he turned back, at

Martin Frobisher

Sir Humphrey Gilbert

the threshold of what would have been his most important discovery.

After Frobisher, more than a hundred expeditions were undertaken to find the northwest passage. While these adventurers were hunting for it they also hunted the whale, the walrus, and the seal.

Ten years after Frobisher, John Davis, another Englishman, made three voyages to search the waters between Greenland on the east and

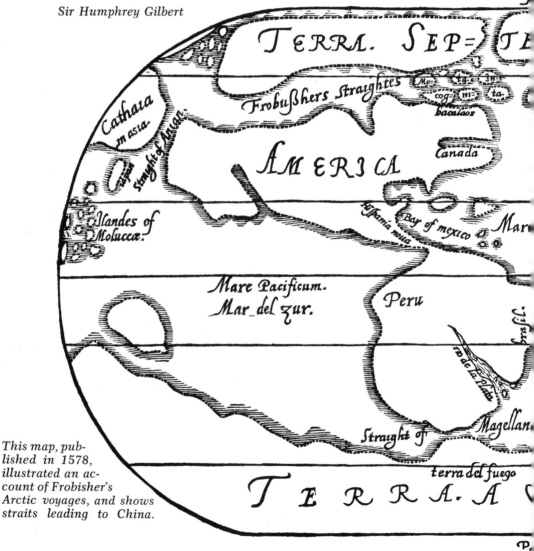

This map, published in 1578, illustrated an account of Frobisher's Arctic voyages, and shows straits leading to China.

the chain of large arctic islands on the west, the great channel that is called Davis Strait. He also saw the entrance to Hudson Strait, which leads into Hudson Bay, but because of the "furious overfall," as he called it, or clash of crosscurrents at that point—"the water whirling and roring as it were the meeting of tides"—he did not venture inside.

Fifteen years after Davis, a third Englishman, George Waymouth, did

Henry Hudson

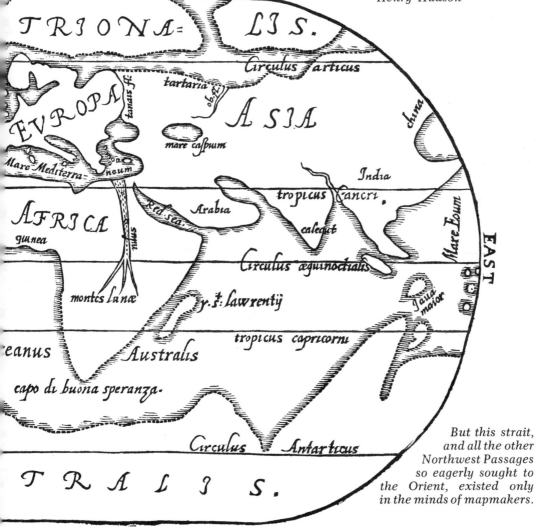

But this strait, and all the other Northwest Passages so eagerly sought to the Orient, existed only in the minds of mapmakers.

This Dutch map of 1635 (with West at top) shows the "Noord Rivier" (the North or Hudson River) up which Henry Hudson sailed in 1609, seeking a Northwest Passage.

enter Hudson Strait and sailed more than halfway through the 450-mile channel towards Hudson Bay. He was defeated when his crew, terrified by the ice, turned back.

The gropings in those ice-laden seas were not wholly in vain; the information they brought back, the charts they made, led to one of the most important discoveries in America's history—the venture of Henry Hudson into the great bay (an inland sea of nearly twice the area of Texas) that is named after him.

Hudson spent all his years as an explorer trying to find a short way to China. He was convinced one could reach the Orient from Europe by sailing along the northern rim of the land either to the east or west. He began by seeking a north*east* passage along the coast of Russia and Siberia. Twice he failed, the second time when his crew, led by the mate, Robert Juet, forced him to turn back.

For his third attempt he switched from his English backers to sail for the Dutch East India Company. From Holland he embarked in 1609 in the tiny ship *Half Moon* with a crew of 20 men. Once more Hudson started out for the northeast. However, when he found himself blocked by the huge ice-clad land of Nova Zembla, north of Russia, and his men once more began to grumble, he gave up trying to find a way around it, reversed his course and crossed the Atlantic to look for the passage to the Indies through America.

The *Half Moon* sailed down the coast to Chesapeake Bay, then turned back north. On September 11, 1609,

she entered the upper bay, now called New York Harbor, the first European ship known to do so since the visit of Verrazano eighty-five years before.

Hudson proceeded into the great river that bears his name, sailed upstream 150 miles, and then went on in a boat a few miles farther. The red and gold of autumn foliage and the clear, fresh beauty of the valley, the broad river, the palisade-like cliffs, and the Catskills enthralled him. But the farther he went the clearer also was the truth that he had not found a way to the Pacific.

Hudson sailed his ship, the Half Moon, *up the river named after him. Near present-day Albany—where Indians rowed out to greet him—he decided to turn back.*

Along the river he found the Indians to be "very loving people"—something that could not be said of his own men, who had murdered several of them along the way. When the Indians thought Hudson was afraid of their bows and arrows "they broke them in pieces and threw them into the fire." They brought beaver and otter skins to the *Half Moon*, which they traded for beads, knives, and hatchets.

When the news of these dealings in furs got back to Holland there was a rush of Dutch ships to this place and the colony of New Amsterdam sprang into being.

Now the British government demanded that Hudson carry on any further explorations for his own country, not for Holland. The next year, therefore, he set out from England for the American arctic to see if he could extend the inland penetrations that had been made by Frobisher, Davis, Waymouth, and other British navigators.

Using Waymouth's ship, the *Discovery*, and the charts of his predecessors, Hudson sailed directly to the turbulent waters of the strait that had terrified Waymouth's crew.

Heavy veils of summer fog hung over the strait—an eerie world of desolate shores, menacing cliffs and great floes and icebergs.

On the third of August, 1610, to Hudson's delight he saw the five-mile-wide strait widen into a great sea beyond the limits of his sight—open water that, for all he knew, might extend westward to China. It was Hudson Bay!

Back and forth the *Discovery* plied, seeking a way out of the shallow waters of James Bay to the south, but there was no strait. After several weeks the men protested.

The spokesman for the defiant crew was Robert Juet. Juet had been guilty of insubordinate conduct on all three of Hudson's previous voyages, and yet, Hudson had taken him again as mate. Standing with Juet was a young man named Henry Greene, who declared he "would rather be hanged at home than starved abroad."

Hoping to stave off a mutiny, Hudson demoted Juet and named another man as the mate. He continued the futile search for a channel until winter set in. Then he beached the ship and dug in for the season.

With the coming of spring in June, Hudson wanted to continue his quest of the westward water route. His plans were thwarted within a few days, however, when open mutiny broke out.

Led by Juet and Greene, a majority of the crew took over command of the *Discovery*. Hudson and six others were forced into the boat, which the ship had in tow.

At this point the ship's carpenter turned against the mutineers and got into the boat with Hudson. He told the mutineers he "knew wat side God stood upon."

Sailors tow their ship through ice-floes in this Dutch engraving made in 1598. The Discovery *must have looked much like this as Hudson entered Hudson Bay.*

As the boat with Hudson and his faithful shipmates bobbed along at the end of the towline through the silent, lonely vastness, a figure appeared at the stern of the *Discovery*, a man with an axe. The axe was raised and brought down on the towline—and the eight men were left behind to die.

The *Discovery* sailed safely home. But Henry Greene was killed by an Eskimo when he went ashore and tried to steal food belonging to the natives, and Juet died of starvation.

That Hudson was deliberately abandoned in those remote waters is known because one of the nine survivors who reached England told the whole story. What lay to the west of that great inland sea he had seen —whether the open water reached all the way to the Pacific—he could not say because the *Discovery* had not explored to the west. But a sea it was, of immense area.

All England was thrilled by this report, which made it seem certain that an English ship had at last found the Northwest Passage. By law, the mutineers who returned should have been hanged for their crime. But they were not punished. They were the only men who had sailed the sea that was thought to lead to the Indies. Their knowledge was too valuable to destroy.

THE GREAT RIVER

In the 1660's most of the coast line of America was known. And yet, the map makers of Europe still believed a passage could be found for ships to sail through this new world and on to the Indies. Explorers were still trying to find out.

The British had already settled a large part of New England. They had taken the colony of New Netherland from the Dutch and renamed it New York. And to the south they were pushing into the interior from Virginia. Still farther south, immense areas of the two continents were under the domination of New Spain.

But the share of America that Samuel Champlain had worked so hard to win for France by founding the colony of Quebec was dwindling. The Iroquois, bitter enemies of New France, were trading with the British and the Dutch, and repeatedly attacking French settlements.

At last, in 1665, France decided a foothold in America was worth fighting for. An army was sent to Quebec, strong enough to overwhelm the whole Iroquois nation. Within a few months this enemy of New France was forced to sue for peace.

In January, 1680, on his exploration into the interior, La Salle stopped at a village of friendly Illinois Indians.

With the enemy thus removed, there followed a great spreading-out over the north-central part of the country of adventurers, traders, and missionaries from New France. They set up outposts at key points and laid claim to the land. Their grand ob-

134

The Indians fed La Salle's party, and rubbed their feet with bear grease. Next, La Salle made the Indians a present of some hatchets and tobacco. Soon after, Fort Crèvecoeur was built nearby, by the La Salle party, on the Illinois River.

jective was to build a powerful empire in America that would control the main routes of commerce and especially—if they could find it— the long-sought transcontinental water route to the Pacific.

One of the most venturesome of these pathfinders was a Canadian-born Frenchman named Louis Jolliet. He had traded for many years among the Indians. He knew how to find his way through the heavy north woods and how to manage a canoe in rough waters.

135

In 1672, Louis Jolliet and Père Marquette descended the Mississippi in canoes.

Father Jacques Marquette

René Robert Cavelier, Sieur de La Salle

Louis Jolliet

In 1669, Jolliet set out from Quebec to search for copper mines that were thought to exist on the shore of Lake Superior. He went as far as Sault Sainte Marie, on the Upper Peninsula of the present state of Michigan, where the waters of Lake Superior fall into Lake Huron.

There Jolliet met a young Jesuit, Father Jacques Marquette. Marquette had selected Sault Sainte Marie as the site of a mission, one of a chain of such stations which were being established through the lake country by French priests.

From the Indians Marquette had learned of the existence of a "great river," not far from Sault Sainte Marie, that arose somewhere to the north and flowed southward all the way to the sea. He told Jolliet about it. Jolliet returned to Quebec, but in the autumn of 1672 he set out again to see if he could find the river. In May, 1673, Jolliet and Marquette, with five other men in two birch bark canoes, began their search.

They went to Green Bay, the large arm of Lake Michigan to the west. The Indians, anxious to keep up their trading with Jolliet, tried to prevent the French from traveling further. Horrible demons would swallow up men and canoes together, the Indians told them.

But the French pushed on. By strenuous paddling and portaging, the six hard-muscled woodsmen and their equally rugged chaplain made their way upstream along the Fox River to the Wisconsin River. There, as Marquette wrote, "We left the waters flowing to Quebec to float on those that would take us through strange lands."

At last, on June 17, 1673, near the present town of Prairie du Chien, Wisconsin, in wonderment and joy which they "could not express," they saw before them the Mississippi. As the canoes glided into the mighty stream, Jolliet felt sure he had found the western waterway, and was now on his way to California and the Pacific Ocean.

It was a rich, untouched country they had entered. As they paddled down the "father of waters," with the current helping them along, they were filled with delight by the widening valley and the abundance of deer and other living things.

One of the canoes almost collided with a catfish. It was so big—wrote Marquette—that it almost overturned the boat.

Friendly Indians entertained the Frenchmen and gave them a calumet, or pipe of peace. Many times

This famous landmark—an Indian painting known as the "Piasaw Monster"— has now vanished; but Marquette and Jolliet must have seen it on the bluffs at Alton, Illinois, just north of the junction of the Missouri with the Mississippi.

after that they were able to avoid trouble with less trusting tribes by bringing out the pipe.

Jolliet was puzzled, however, by the course of the river. To reach the Gulf of California he knew it would have to make a long lap westward. But the main course continued steadily south.

Near the location of the modern city of St. Louis he was astonished to see another vast stream joining the Mississippi. This was the Missouri. After talking with the Indians, Jolliet was convinced that the Missouri would take them westward to California—which it would not have done—and that the Mississippi

At the point where the Arkansas joins the Mississippi, Marquette and Jolliet turned back. Ten years later, in 1682, when La Salle was descending the river, he stopped here, erected a cross, and continued south to the Gulf of Mexico.

sippi. There he held another parley with the Indians. He was told that ten more days of canoeing would bring him to the Gulf but was warned against going on. The tribes to the south were warlike and had guns— given to them by the Spaniards.

Jolliet saw no point in continuing only to be captured by those natives or by the Spaniards themselves. He turned back, and after a grueling journey upstream, reached Quebec the following summer.

Five years before Marquette and Jolliet started down the Mississippi another adventurer—a young fur trader on the St. Lawrence who was destined to become the greatest pioneer in the America of his time—had been planning to find and explore the great river himself.

Robert Cavelier de La Salle, son of a wealthy merchânt in France, came to America in 1666 to take over an estate near Montreal which had been granted him by the King. La Salle's neighbors mockingly nicknamed his estate "La Chine" (China) because of his often repeated insistence that a way could be found for ships to get through to China.

La Salle wanted to strike inland from New France towards the south and west to examine the country be-

flowed not to the Pacific but to the Gulf of Mexico—which it did. Nevertheless, he decided to continue down the Mississippi.

A few days later, where Cairo, Illinois, stands today, he saw the mouth of the Ohio. Proceeding south, he stopped where the Arkansas River empties into the Missis-

tween the Great Lakes and Mexico. If he found good furs there, he wanted to set up trading posts and stake out a claim for New France to this huge sector of the American interior. He would protect that claim with a chain of forts. And if the passage to China lay through the interior, he wanted to be the man to find it.

His hopes were raised when some Indians from the west visited him at La Chine. They talked about a "great river" that flowed through the middle of the continent to the Vermilion Sea (the Gulf of California), "cutting the land in two." To reach the river, they said, La Salle must go by canoe to Lake Erie and make a three-day portage.

Like Jolliet, La Salle believed the river must run to the south and west and that it must empty into the Gulf of California. If so, then here, indeed, lay the way by water to the Indies! Greatly excited, he sold his estate at La Chine to finance an expedition, and in the summer of 1669 set out to find the river with a group of Indian guides.

Failing to find the Mississippi, he roamed the country, talked with the Indians, and learned all he could about how the land lay. In 1673 he was back in Quebec.

The next several years he spent doing everything he could to promote the fur trade. The King of France granted him a monopoly on this business in the Mississippi Val-

ley. He set up trading posts in western New York State, on Lake Michigan, and on the Illinois River, and he built ships to speed up the transporation of furs over inland waters.

Yet he never gave up the hope of some day tracing the Mississippi down to the sea. After Louis Jolliet returned from his exploration, 1674, the river was known down to the point where it was joined by the Arkansas. La Salle now knew that the Mississippi was not a passage to China; but by going down the whole length to the Gulf of Mexico, he could claim for France the river and the huge valley through which it flowed. He could found a great French empire in the very heart of America.

In January, 1680, La Salle established a post on the Illinois River near the southern end of Lake Michigan. Because of the many discouragements he met with there, he would one day call it Fort Crèvecoeur —"Fort Heartbreak."

As soon as it was finished he began building a ship of forty tons in which he hoped to make the journey down the Illinois to the Mississippi and then on down to the Gulf. But the vessel could not be completed without more equipment and supplies. For this reason, and also because he wanted news of his other business operations, La Salle decided to go back to the fort he had established at Niagara, in western New York State—a journey of a thousand miles.

The rivers and lakes were still frozen over. He could not make any part of the journey by canoe. Yet the way by land was very hard too, because it was overlaid by a thick blanket of soft snow that would not support snowshoes.

After this trip—certainly one of the hardest ever made through the American wilderness—La Salle had to go back two more times to the Illinois country to meet emergencies that arose at his trading posts because of new outbreaks of Indian warfare.

Two years passed. During this time the Iroquois, who were at war with La Salle's friends, the Illinois, attacked Fort Crèvecoeur and left both the settlement and the unfinished ship in ashes.

At last, however, in January, 1682, he was ready to attempt the journey with a small fleet of canoes. He took with him twenty-three Frenchmen, eighteen Indian warriors, ten squaws, and three children.

From Lake Michigan the party set out through the ice and snow, dragging their canoes and supplies over the "Chicago portage" to the Illinois River. From the ruins of Fort Crèvecoeur they put out into the river in their canoes.

As La Salle's party descended the Mississippi, they decided to name it the "Colbert" River, after the chief minister of the French king, Louis XIV.

On April 9, 1682, La Salle reached the mouth of the Mississippi. Here he claimed the river, and the lands it drained, for the Bourbon king, Louis XIV of France.

Where it joined the Mississippi, the Illinois was clogged with ice. The little fleet had to wait a week for it to break up. Once through it, the canoes shot down the great river under the double push of current and strong-armed Indian paddlers.

When the Frenchmen approached the Gulf of Mexico they ran short of food because they could not hunt animals in the marshes of the delta. The Indians brought them meat which they found peculiarly "good and delicate"—until they learned it was human flesh.

"Advancing on," a priest in the party wrote, "we discovered the open sea, so that on the ninth of April [1682] with all possible solemnity, we performed the ceremony of planting the cross and raising the arms of France. After we had chanted hymns . . . the Sieur de La Salle, in the name of His Majesty, took possession of

La Salle named the huge French territory Louisiana, in honor of his king.

tlement between Florida and Mexico, a few hundred miles above the mouth of the Mississippi.

When he returned to America two years later with 400 colonists and soldiers, in 1684, he chose to sail into the Gulf of Mexico and enter the Mississippi Valley from the southern end.

He missed the mouth of the river, however, and landed far to the west, at Matagorda Bay, Texas. There he built Fort St. Louis, and planted his colony. But it was to be a failure.

In January, 1687, starvation and disease had killed all but forty-one of La Salle's men. Their situation was so desperate that La Salle and sixteen others decided to try to reach the distant Illinois country and get help. On their way north through Texas, while the party was hunting buffalo, La Salle got into an argument with his men over food supplies. One of his own men shot him from ambush.

Thus, in a stupid quarrel, the life of the great explorer was ended, on March 19, 1687.

that river, of all the rivers that enter it, and of all the country watered by them."

Hoping to solidify the French claim to the whole Mississippi Valley, La Salle went back to France and sought men and finances for a colony in the territory he had just opened. King Louis XIV of France approved his plan for founding a set-

In 1687, La Salle was murdered in Texas.

THE LAST CORNER

When Martin Frobisher returned to England from his first voyage across the Atlantic, not even he knew that the "passage to the Indies," which he claimed to have discovered in the far north of America, was really the long inlet known today as Frobisher Bay.

His story found an eager listener in the person of a tough, fearless sea raider named Francis Drake. Drake had conceived a bold plan to sail into the Pacific and raid Spanish ships that were carrying huge treasures of gold and silver out of Peru. Now, if it was indeed a strait that Frobisher had discovered, Drake realized that it could be entered from the Pacific Ocean as well as from the Atlantic. And if Drake succeeded in raiding Spanish treasure galleons in the Pacific, possibly he could make his way home by way of Frobisher's strait.

Drake sailed from England late in the year 1577, and passed into the Pacific through the Strait of Magellan. He plundered Spanish vessels in the ports of Arica and Callao, and overtook a treasure ship off the coast of Peru. Her cargo, which he captured, was worth about $5,000,000 in today's money.

Continuing northward according to plan, he began the search for the waterway to the Atlantic.

Many years before, Spanish sailors had explored the west coast perhaps as far up as Oregon. But this did not prevent Drake from going ashore in California, claiming the land for Queen Elizabeth, and calling it Nova Albion (New England). He sank a post in the earth bearing a plate of

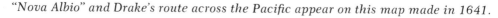

"Nova Albio" and Drake's route across the Pacific appear on this map made in 1641.

brass on which were engraved the Queen's name, the date of his landing, June 17, 1579, and an English claim to the whole country. To add the Queen's portrait and her coat of arms, he imbedded a silver sixpence in the plate.

This done, Drake resumed his search for the strait. But after exploring the coast almost to the mouth of the Columbia River and groping through "most vile, thick and stinking fogs," he gave it up. To go back the way he had come would have meant risking capture by Spanish ships of war. Instead, he set his course westward across the Pacific and in 1580 reached Plymouth, England—the second man in history to sail around the world.

The part of the world where east meets west, where only 56 miles of water separate eastern Siberia from

When Sir Francis Drake (above) docked in Plymouth, England, in 1580, at the close of his world voyage, Queen Elizabeth was so delighted to learn of his plundering the treasure cities of New Spain that she boarded his ship, the Golden Hind, (below) and knighted him.

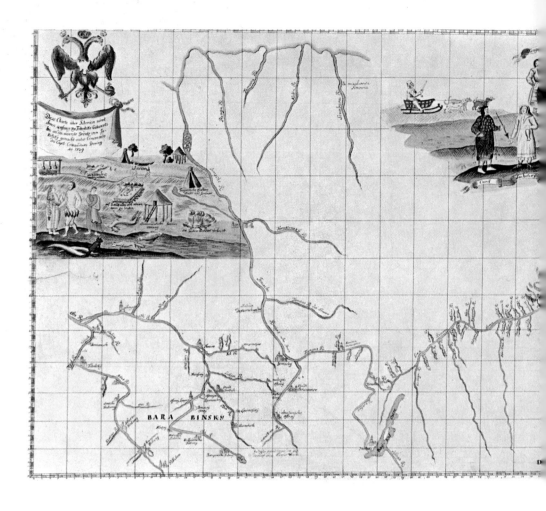

This Russian map, made in 1735, shows the route of Bering's five-year expedition. Two of the Siberian tribesmen pictured here are seen mounted on reindeer.

western Alaska, remained wholly unknown to Europeans for another hundred and fifty years.

Then, the most enterprising of all the czars of Russia—Peter the Great—grew eager to expand his empire into the eastern limits of Siberia, and also to learn whether or not the easternmost shore of Asia was joined to the western tip of North America.

To accomplish this, he planned to launch a ship from the great Siberian peninsula of Kamchatka. But Kamchatka, jutting into the Pacific Ocean, was 5,000 miles from St. Petersburg. Much of the way lay through a trackless wilderness beyond the easternmost outposts of the Siberian fur traders. Even to get there from Russia—to say nothing of transporting the tools and materials for building a ship—would be a superhuman feat.

Before the expedition could get under way, Peter was dead. But his widow, Empress Catherine, decided

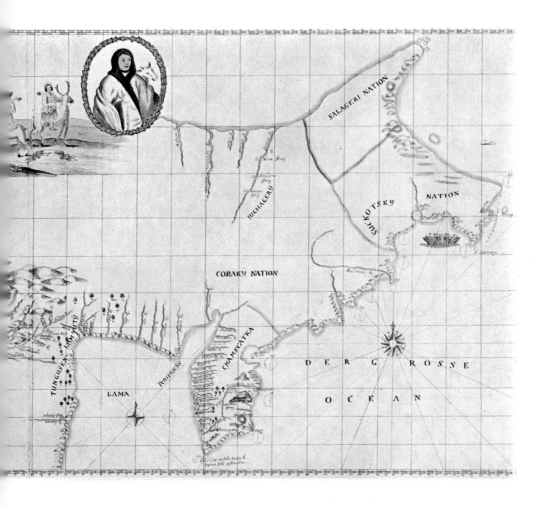

The peninsula labeled "Chamscatka" is the Kamchatka, where Bering built the
St. Gabriel *and sailed through the Straits of Anian (later called Bering Strait).*

to have his plan carried out. In 1724 the mighty task was assigned to Vitus Bering, a Danish sea captain who had helped Czar Peter build the Russian Navy.

After more than three years of hardship and back breaking labor, Bering managed to reach the shore of Kamchatka and there build a 60-foot sailing vessel. He named her the *St. Gabriel.*

He set sail in the summer of 1728. For a month he proceeded north, closely following the coast of the Asiatic mainland. Much of the journey was made through fog. On August 14, the Siberian shoreline fell sharply away to the west, leaving open sea ahead. He continued on his northward course two more days, still with no land in sight.

Since he had sailed to latitude 67° 18′, Bering had actually crossed the Arctic Circle, passed through the strait between Alaska and Siberia—which was later given his name—

Vitus Jonassen Bering.

Bering arrived back in St. Petersburg in the spring of 1730—five years after his departure. Geographers for the Russian government refused to believe that the explorer had sailed through waters separating Asia from America.

Their skepticism so angered Bering that he obtained permission in 1733 to make the trek to Kamchatka again and explore further. This time Bering built two more ships and sailed across the North Pacific to the coast of Alaska. Weary, 60 years old, and sick, he had no sooner sent his men ashore to get water than he ordered them back aboard ship to start for home—probably because the dreaded scurvy had begun to show among them. His ship, the *St. Peter*, ran into fierce storms. She was driven into a cove off an island 100 miles from Kamchatka. Shortly after her crew went ashore, a fierce storm smashed her to bits. A few weeks later, in December, 1741, Bering died in a rude shelter on what is now known as Bering Island.

Many men still cast doubts on Bering's discovery—doubts which were not to be stilled until 1778, when the Englishman, Captain Cook, passed through Bering Strait, rounded East Cape, and sailed westward along the northern Siberian coast.

Now the farthest corner of the great land mass of America had been rounded by men in ships. All of it could be pictured by map makers.

and into the Arctic Sea. Had the weather been clear at the time, he could have seen both east and west shores, Alaska to his right, Siberia to his left.

Seeing nothing, and nearing the end of a short summer season in a tiny vessel that was not built to withstand the storms of an Arctic winter, Bering turned back. He believed he had gone beyond the northernmost point of the Siberian shore, and therefore assumed that Asia and America were not connected by land. His guess was correct, but since fogs had prevented him from verifying his finding, his discovery remained in doubt.

At last, the picture in men's minds of the shape of the land, the knowledge that had begun to grow from the finding of a tiny island in the Sea of Darkness on the morning of October 12, 1492, was clear in its main outlines.

It had taken 300 years for those outlines to be drawn without guesswork. The adventurous men who had pieced out those coast lines—Columbus, Cabot, Drake, Bering, and all the rest—had usually failed to find the things they were looking for. Yet out of their individual failures came a greater success, something bigger than any one of them could have dreamed of, something better than anything they were seeking. For each of these men, by adding the work of his own life to that of all the others, had helped in solving the greatest secret on earth—the secret of America.

Bering died in 1741 on Bering Island, in the Commander Islands, off Kamchatka.

APPENDIX

ACKNOWLEDGMENTS: The editors are deeply grateful to Lawrence C. Wroth for giving generously of his knowledge of discoverers of the New World and for his guidance and advice; and to Gertrudis Feliu, Chief of the European Bureau for HORIZON, for giving so much of her valuable time and assistance in obtaining rare material from the Bibliotheque Nationale and other sources in Paris. In addition, they wish expressly to thank the following individuals and organizations for their generous assistance, and for their cooperation in furnishing pictorial material from their collections; Mrs. Maud D. Cole, Mr.

Lewis M. Stark—Rare Book Division, New York Public Library; Dr. Gordon F. Ekholm—American Museum of Natural History; Miss Roberta Paine, Miss Lillian Green, Dr. Randolph Bullock—Metropolitan Museum of Art; Miss Dorothy Bowen, Mr. Robert O. Dougan—Henry E. Huntington Library and Art Gallery, San Marino, Calif.; Mrs. David W. Knepper—San Jacinto Museum of History; Mr. John Parker—James Ford Bell Collection, University of Minnesota; Mr. Merritt S. Hitt—City Art Museum of St. Louis.

PICTURE CREDITS

The source of each picture used in this book is listed below, by page. When two or more pictures appear on one page, they are separated by semicolons. The following abbreviations are used.

AMNH—American Museum of Natural History, New York
BL—Bodleian Library, Oxford, England
BM—Trustees of the British Museum, London, England
BN—Bibliotheque Nationale, Paris, France
HL—Huntington Library, San Marino, California
JCBL—John Carter Brown Library, Providence, Rhode Island
JFBC—James Ford Bell Collection, University of Minnesota Library
KG—Kennedy Galleries, New York
KM—Kunsthistorische Museum, Vienna, Austria

MMA—Courtesy of the Metropolitan Museum of Art
N—Nationalbibliothek, Vienna, Austria
NMFA—National Museum of Fine Arts, Madrid, Spain
NMM—National Maritime Museum, Greenwich, England
NYHS—New York Historical Society
PL—Collection of the Duke of Alba, Palacio de Liria, Madrid, Spain
PM—Peabody Museum, Harvard University
RBD–NYPL—Rare Book Division, New York Public Library
UG—Uffizi Gallery, Gioviana Collection, Florence, Italy

Cover: "Columbus at Hispaniola," an engraving by T. De Bry, from *India Occidentalis*, 1590, RBD-NYPL. **Front end sheet:** Manuscript Div., NYPL. **Half title:** Detail from Joannes Martines' 1578 Map of Cibola, BM. **Title:** (l. to. r.) Warren Clifton Shearman Coll.; JFBC; Thomas W. Streeter Coll.; RBD-NYPL; American Heritage Coll.; RBD-NYPL. **Contents:** *Light of Navigation*, Blaeu, 1622, Library of Congress. **11** BL. **12** (top) *Geschichte des Zeitalters*, Ruge, 1881, NYPL; (bot.) *Book of Ser Marco Polo*, ed. Yule, 1871, NYPL. **13** Macpherson Coll., NMM. **14** (top) BN; (bot.) *Livre des Merveilles*, 1375, BN. **15** BN. **16** (top) *Cousas Raras da India*, 1558, Pierpont Morgan Library; (bot.) *Civitates Orbus Terrarum*, Braun, 1576, RBD-NYPL. **18** MMA, Gift of J. Pierpont Morgan, 1900. **19** (top l.) *Geschichte des Zeitalters*, Ruge, 1881, NYPL; (top r.) *His Book of Privileges*, Columbus, RBD-NYPL; (bot.) Warren Clifton Shearman Coll. **20** *Hist. of Amer.*, Winsor, Vol. II, 1886. **21** Columbus' Letter to Sanchez, 1493, RBD-NYPL. **23** BN. **24** (top) *Warhafftige Historia*, Hans Staden, 1557, RBD-NYPL; (bot.) *The Seaman's Secrets*, John Davys, 1595, RBD-NYPL. **25** Coll. of Capt. Eric C. Palmer, England. **26** (top) Map Div., NYPL; (bot.) *Historia General*, Herrera, 1601, RBD-NYPL. **27** op. cit. **28** Map Div., NYPL. **30** Columbus' Letter to Sanchez, 1493, RBD-NYPL. **31** op. cit. **32** *India Occidentalis*, De Bry, 1590, RBD-NYPL. **34** Stokes Coll., NYPL. **35** (all) *La Historia*, Benzoni, 1572, RBD-NYPL. **36** (top l.) from a painting by Pinturicchio, Vatican Library; (top r.) KM; (bot. both) NMFA.

38 BN. **39** NYHS. **40** (top) JFBC; (bot.) *Lalettera*, Dati, 1493, RBD-NYPL. **41** *Cosmographiae introductio*, Waldseemüller, 1507, RBD-NYPL. **42** *India Occidentalis*, De Bry, 1590, RBD-NYPL. **44** UG. **45** *America*, Part X, De Bry, RBD-NYPL. **46** *India Occidentalis*, De Bry, 1590, RBD-NYPL. **48** *Historia General*, Herrera, 1601, RBD-NYPL. **49** *India Occidentalis*, De Bry, 1590, RBD-NYPL. **52** Warren Clifton Shearman Coll. **53** UG. **54** BM. **56–57** (cen.) PL. **56** (l.) *Premier Voyage autour du monde*, Pigafetta, 1801, RBD-NYPL. **57** (r.) op. cit. **58** *Johann Schoner*, Coote, 1888, RBD-NYPL. **59** *Voyages*, Hulsius, 1603, RBD-NYPL. **60** JCBL. **62** *Voyages*, Hulsius, 1603, RBD-NYPL. **63** (r.) op. cit.; (l.) *The Great Age of Discovery*, Paul Herrmann, NYPL. **65** *India Occidentalis*, 1590, RBD-NYPL. **66** *Coleccion de los Viages*, Navarrete, NYPL. **67** (both) *Historia General*, Herrera, 1728, RBD-NYPL. **68** BM. **69** (both) B.M. **70** Moliner Coll., photo by "Giraudon," Paris; **71** (l. & r.) *Historia General*, Herrera, 1728, RBD-NYPL. **71** (cen.) *Retratos de los Espanoles Illustre*, 1791, NYPL. **72** BN. **73** (both) AMNH. **74** (top) *Codex Telleriano*, BN; (bot.) Andre Emmerech Gallery, AMNH. **75** (top) BN; (bot.) HL. **76** (top) *Lienzo de Tlazcalla*, NYPL; (bot.) AMNH. **77** AMNH. **78** *India Occidentalis*, De Bry, 1590, RBD-NYPL. **80** *Guaman Poma de Ayala*, NYPL. **81** (top) op. cit.; (bot.) Old Print Shop. **82** *Codex Telleriano*, BN. **83** NYHS. **84–85** Map drawn expressly for this book by Elmer Smith. **87** *India Occidentalis*, De Bry, 1590, RBD-NYPL. **88** *Les singularitez de la France Antarctique*, Thevet, 1558, RBD-NYPL.

89 (all) San Jacinto Museum of History, Texas. 90 (all) MMA, (sword, burganet, breastplate— Gift of William H. Riggs, 1913) (shirt of mail— The Bashford Dean Memorial Coll., Purchase 1929, Funds from various donors). 91 N. 92–93 Map drawn expressly for this book by Elmer Smith. 94 Frederic Remington. 95 *India Occidentalis*, De Bry, 1590, RBD-NYPL. 96 Andreas Feininger. 97 Peter Hurd, 1937, Roswell Museum & Art Gallery, New Mexico. 98 BM. 101 Smithsonian Institute. 102 Ray Manley, Shostal. 104 Wisconsin State Historical Society. 106 (top) BM; (bot.) Bushnell Coll., PM. 107 op. cit. 108 op. cit. 109 *Histoire des Yncas*, Garcilaso de la Vega, 1737, RBD-NYPL. 110 Frederic Remington. 112 *Historiae Canadensis*, Du Creux, 1664, RBD-NYPL. 113 *Les Raretés des Indes*, NYPL. 114 Marquise de Villefranche, Paris. 115 HL. 116 *Delle Navigation et Viaggi*, Ramusio, 1606, RBD-NYPL. 117 op. cit. 118 *Orbis Habitabilis*, Carolus Allard, 1690, RBD-NYPL. 120 Print Div., NYPL. 121 *Voyages*, Champlain, 1632, RBD-NYPL. 122 BN. 124 *Les Voyages*, Champlain, 1613, RBD-NYPL. 125 op. cit. 126 BM. 127 BL. 128 (top) *Collectio· of Voyages and Travels*, John Harris, 1705, RBD-NYPL. 128–129 (cen.) *A true discourse*, George Best, 1578, RBD-NYPL. 129 (top) Art Commission of the City of New York. 131 Owen, Black Star. 133 *Diarium nauticum*, Gerrit de Veer, 1598, RBD-NYPL. 135 KG. 136 (top to bot.) NYPL; NYPL; Rouen Library; Public Archives of Canada. 137 City Art Museum, St. Louis. 138 KG. 141 KG. 142 KG. 143 KG. 144 *Voyage de F. Drach*, Hakluyt, 1641, RBD-NYPL. 145 (top) NMM; (bot.) *Vikings of the Pacific*, A. C. Laut, c. 1905, With permission of the Macmillan Co. 146 JFBC. 148 *Den Slora Expeditionen*, Swen Waxell, NYPL. 149 NMM. 50 *America*, Part IV, De Bry, RBD-NYPL. Back end sheet: map by J. B. Nolin, Old Print Shop.

FOR FURTHER READING

Young readers seeking further information on Discoverers of the New World will find the following books to be both helpful and entertaining:

Adams, Randolph. *Gateway to History.* New York: Ungar, 1960

Bakeless, John. *The Eyes of Discovery.* Philadelphia: J. B. Lippincott Co., 1950.

Costain, Thomas B. *The White and the Gold.* New York: Doubleday & Co. ,1954.

Debenham, Frank. *The Global Atlas.* New York: Golden Press, 1958.

Garst, Shannon. *Three Conquistadors: Cortes, Coronado, Pizarro.* New York: Messner, 1948.

Kjelgaard, James. *The Explorations of Pere Marquette.* New York: Random House, 1951.

Lamb, Harold. *New Found World.* New York: Doubleday & Co., 1955.

Leithauser, Joachim. *Worlds Beyond the Horizon.* New York: Alfred A. Knopf, 1955.

Morison, Samuel Eliot. *Christopher Columbus, Mariner.* Boston: Little, Brown, 1955

Pond, Seymour. *Ferdinand Magellan.* New York: Random House, 1957.

Riesenberg, Felix. *Balboa: Swordsman and Conquistador.* New York: Messner, 1948.

Sperry, Armstrong. *The Voyages of Christopher Columbus.* New York: Random House, 1950.

Walsh, Richard. (ed.). *The Adventures of Marco Polo.* New York: John Day, 1948.

BIBLIOGRAPHY

Asher, G. M. *Henry Hudson, the Navigator* London: Hakluyt Society, 1860.

Bacchiani, Alessandro. *Giovanni Da Verrazzano and His Discoveries in North America, 1524 According to the unpublished contemporaneous Cellere Codex of Rome, Italy.* Albany: Fifteenth Annual Report of American Scenic and Historic Preservation Society, State of New York, No. 60, 1910.

Beazley, Charles Raymond. *The Dawn of Modern Geography.* Oxford: Oxford University Press, 1897–1906.

Biggar, H. P. *The Voyages of Jacques Cartier.* Ottawa: F. A. Acland, 1924.

Biggar, H. P. (ed.). *The Works of Samuel de Champlain.* Toronto: The Champlain Society, 1925.

Bishop, Morris. *The Odyssey of Cabeza de Vaca.* New York: The Century Co., 1933.

Brebner, John Bartlet. *The Explorers of North America, 1492–1806.* New York: Doubleday & Co., 1955.

Burrage, Henry S. (ed.). *Early English and French Voyages, 1534–1608.* New York: Barnes & Noble, 1906.

Collinson, Richard. *The Three Voyages of Martin Frobisher, in Search of a Passage to Cathaia and India by the Northwest, A. D. 1576–78.* London: Hakluyt Society, 1867.

Colon, Fernando. *The Life of the Admiral Christopher Columbus by his son, Ferdinand.* Translated and annotated by Benjamin Keen. New Brunswick: Rutgers University Press, 1959.

Fiske, John. *The Discovery of America.* Boston: Houghton Mifflin, 1892.

Fletcher, Francis Master. *The World Encompassed by Sir Francis Drake.* London: G. Miller, 1628.

Hammond, George P., and Rey, Agapito. *Narratives of the Coronado Expedition, 1540–1542.* Albuquerque, New Mexico: University of New Mexico Press, 1940.

Harrisse, Henry. *Discovery of North America.* London: Aldine Press, 1892.

Herrera y Tordesillas, Antonio de. *The General History of the Vast Continent and Islands of America.* Translated by Captain John Stevens. London: J. Batley, 1725.

Herrmann, Paul. *The Great Age of Discovery.* Translated by Arnold J. Pomerans. New York: Harper & Brothers, 1958.

Hodge, F. W., and Lewis T. H. (ed.). *Spanish Explorers in the Southern United States, 1528–1543.* New York: Barnes & Noble, 1907.

Horgan, Paul. *Great River, The Rio Grande in North American History.* New York: Rinehart & Co., Inc., 1954.

Idell, Albert. (ed.). *The Bernal Diaz Chronicles.* New York: Doubleday & Co.,1956.

Kellogg, Louise P. (ed.). *Early Narratives of the Northwest, 1634–1699.* New York: Barnes & Noble, 1917.

Komroff, Manuel. (ed.). *The Travels of Marco Polo.* New York: Liveright, 1926.

Lavender, David. *Land of Giants.* New York: Doubleday & Co., 1958.

Markham, Clements R. (ed. and trans.). *The Journal of Christopher Columbus and Documents Relating to the Voyages of John Cabot and Gaspar Corte Real.* London: Hakluyt Society, 1893.

Markham, Clements R. (ed. and trans.). *The Letters of Amerigo Vespucci.* London: Hakluyt Society, 1894.

Morison, Samuel Eliot. *Admiral of the Ocean Sea.* Boston: Little, Brown & Co., 1942.

Narrative of the Career of Hernando de Soto in the Conquest of Florida as told by a Knight of Elvas. Translated by Buckingham Smith. New York: A. S. Barnes, 1904.

Newton, Arthur P. (ed.). *The Great Age of Discovery.* London: University of London Press, 1932.

Parkman, Francis. *The Discovery of the Great West: La Salle.* ed. William R. Taylor. New York: Rinehart, 1956.

Parkman, Francis. *Pioneers of France in the New World.* Boston: Little, Brown & Co., 1913.

Penrose, Boies. *Travel and Discovery in the Renaissance, 1420–1620.* Cambridge: Harvard University Press, 1952.

Prescott, William H. *Conquest of Mexico and Conquest of Peru.* New York: Random House, Modern Library, 1936.

Quintana, Manuel Jose. *Vidas de Espanoles Celebres.* Translated by Margaret Hodson. Edinburgh: 1832.

Stanley, H. E. J. *The First Voyage Round the World.* London: Hakluyt Society, 1847.

Thwaites, Reuben Gold. (ed.). *The Jesuit Relations and Allied Documents: Travels and Explorations of the Jesuit Missionaries in New France, 1610–1791, Vol. LIX.* Cleveland: The Burrows Brothers, 1900.

Webb, W. P. *The Great Plains.* Boston: Ginn & Co., 1931.

Winship, G. P. (ed.). *The Journey of Coronado.* New York: A. S. Barnes, 1904.

Winsor, Justin. (ed.). *Narrative and Critical History of America.* Boston: Houghton Mifflin & Co., 1884.

INDEX

Bold face indicates pages on which maps or illustrations appear

This map was made in 1775—twenty-seven after Bering's voyage of discovery